For Susan Marie,
who does so much for
Buffalo poetry.

Love,

Loren Keller

Also by Loren Keller

POETRY

No Songs But Whispers (1969)

The Skier and the Snow (1978)

Warm Brooms (1979)

As I Might Hold A Bird (1983)

FICTION

Four And Twenty Bluebeards (1999)

PLAYS

What Dreams May Come (1986)

Walt Whitman, Oscar Wilde (1988)

I Am Walt Whitman (1989)

No Spartan Shield (1990)

First Snow, Last Snow (1991)

The Dazzling Traveling Chopin Show (1992)

Blues For Lloca (1993)

The Gift Of The Magi (adaptation) (2001)

It's A Wonderful Life (adaptation) (2002)

EVENING EVERYTHING:

The Collected Poems of Loren Keller

Harborage Press
Fort Myers, Florida
First Edition

ISBN: 9780977052608
ISBN: 0-9770526-0-5
Library of Congress Control Number: 2005929369

Printed in the United States of America
First Edition

This book is for

Michelle and Jamie

Alyse and Jana

Brittany and Dominique

Brandon, Julianne, and Jordan

Table of Contents

THE HOUR BEFORE THE WIND

WARM BROOMS

WILDFLOWERS

THE SKIER AND THE SNOW

AS I MIGHT HOLD A BIRD

EVENING EVERYTHING

Introduction

I have always written poems, even as a small child; but I became seriously involved with poetry after returning to college after three years in the US Army during the Korean War. I won the Poetry Award at Buffalo State in 1955, and went through a kind of "apprenticeship," writing numerous poems but usually being less than satisfied with them. Then, in the early Sixties, I had a breakthrough: I began feeling that my most recent works were, in one word, right.

The Ford Foundation gave me a John Hay Fellowship in 1964 at Cal Berkeley, and I had a wonderful opportunity to concentrate on writing. The immediate result was a group of fifteen poems which I put in a folder marked *The Berkeley Poems*. I had great support from a number of poets in the Bay Area, especially Gary Snyder. When I returned home, I made certain that I set time aside for writing, no matter how busy I was in my teaching job. By 1968 I had poems in several magazines, and felt that I was ready to have my work in a book. *No Songs But Whispers* came out in 1969, and included *The Berkeley Poems*, along with thirty later poems.

In 1977 the death of Michael Sneath, the young son of my good friends George and Beth, caused me to write a long poem, *The Skier and the Snow*, dedicated to Michael. His parents brought out the poem in a lovely little chapbook. Two years later *Warm Brooms* appeared, with the sub-title "Poems 1968-1979." It was my largest book to date, with sixty-eight poems, but I was very aware of leaving out poems that I felt deserved to be included. In my introduction to that volume, I said, "These are a few poems selected from all that I have written since *No Songs But Whispers*."

The only book of my poetry that has come out since then is a small collection of seven poems in 1983 with the title *As I Might*

Hold A Bird. Why twenty years without a book of poetry? My writing became channeled in other directions. Although I continued to write poems at intervals, I was focused on theatre starting with the production of my first play in 1986. I became the Playwright-in-Residence at Buffalo Ensemble Theatre, and eventually five of my plays were produced there and others were given staged readings in various locales.

In the Nineties my literary energies took another turn. I wrote my novel *Four and Twenty Bluebeards*, which came out in 1999, and I began writing essays for the literary magazine *First Intensity*. I continued to give frequent poetry readings, though, and got great support from my fellow poets Ken Feltges and John Milner. When my good friend and former student David Winstel suggested that my Collected Poems should be published, I realized that there were many poems of mine that had never been in book form or even in magazines. And that included poems that were quite familiar to audiences at my readings.

It has been a labor of love, returning to works I had tucked away in folders and boxes. This is a life's work, from 1954 to the present. The titles of the sections of the book are titles I had planned to use for prospective books of poetry, some of which never appeared. I hope you will share my excitement in discovering (or re-discovering) poems that might otherwise have been lost forever. Now they can take their place with the poems from my four earlier books. Welcome to the pages of *Evening Everything*.

Loren

No Songs
But Whispers

The Berkeley Poems

Mc COY TYNER AT THE
JAZZ WORKSHOP

If you couldn't be
piano keys
his fingers touched,

the best thing
in the room to be
was the San Francisco
phone book

he sat on while he played
because the stool was low.

AWAKE

Today I'll waste
the hours of sunlight
in this tall green park.

Last night I dreamed
a field
of bloodless stumps.

Whose amputated woods
those were
I thought I knew,

Whose grey clouds sagged
retching their warm rain
on the stumps.

Awake I'll waste
a day of sunlight
in my tall green park.

I'M HERE

Not morning.
    Sky not even grey, but white.
    I walk. Empty of all
    but emptiness.
    I pass a man with

    -- Argh! Eyes vomit tears
    at what they saw –
    a man with half a face.
    Or less then half.

    Torn by the cold,
    metallic, modern claw.

    The other people passing,
    just like me,
    avert their eyes.
    He is rejected.
    I am not.
    He is not more lost than I.
    No. Lost a different way.
    He has to learn
    how not to hate,
    I how to love.

I want to love him
    but I cannot look.

    One glimpse, involuntary,
    was enough.
    I looked down fast.

    And he must walk this street
    where every passing person
    is a claw
    which tears away another

piece of face
when each, shocked,
looks some other way.
And he hates them,
hates me,
because we turn our heads.

I can love the part
that's missing,
that the claw,
not even wanting,
dropped bloody
in somebody's lap,
his lover's, probably.

He has no lover now.

I love that missing part
because I want
whole faces on the people
that I meet.
Put the part back.

Let me be empty
in comfort, world.
Get the hell out
of my stomach
with your icy claw.
I want him whole,
a recognizable man.

But he'd have other lovers
whole. He wouldn't lack.
Besides, give him a face
and I and everybody else
will pass without a thought.
Give him a face
and he is gone,
absorbed, forgotten.

A shudder may be
kinder than a shrug.

I must love him
with his half-a-face.
Or not at all.
Come back, man.
Scare me to life.
Let me try
to look again.

Or does a stare
claw worse
than an avoiding glance?

If I had loved
before the claw, I would love still,
in spite of it.
Even, I hope,
because of it.

And so perhaps
he has a lover somewhere.
A girl who walks
this street with him
sometimes? Lets others
see her touch
his mangled face?

Feels eyes turned from him
turn from her, too?
I hope to God she does.
That someone does.
But if he never had
a lover,
now he never will.
Unless

Somehow I feel

my wish to love
is almost love itself.
The emptiness
is gone. But what
replaced it
I can't seem to name.

Something is in me.
And it's come
since he passed by.
As if to fill
the emptiness of me
and give my skin
some proof I'm here inside.

Whether I love
or loathe him,
whether next time
I can look,
or only turn away again,
whether it's guilt I feel
or pity,
this I think is true:

I miss him.
And I hurt.
Therefore I am.

AIR

Deeper
and richer
than water
in darkness
the stirless air
surrounds
her solitary
prayer
at the far
altar.

HEMINGWAY'S HAND

The nurse and soldier
touch. They have not
been together often.
We feel love seeding:
the caress and thrust
of what they say.

"Please put your hand
there again."
"It's not been away."

Too early to be merely
tender. Put your hand.
Too tender to be false.
Please there again.

"This is a rotten
game we play…"

Blindly they perceive
by touch. Their game
is shaped by words
and fingers into love:
scene into flesh into art.

The hand
has not been away.

MEDITATION

The room is small.
The wall I face
is glass, much blue.
Sunlight comes
orange crystal red
across my knees,
stops, blue, stops.
Much blue. Comes
red comes clear,
spreads, blue.
Diagonals of crescents
of angles of, blue.

Outside, beyond
broad terraces
of green and air,
light ripples on the surfaces
of San Francisco Bay,
returns in red
from Golden Gate,
comes blinding
yellow orange,
shuts, my eyes.

The lids stop,
olive, much deep grey.
Half open pierced
by silver. Closing,
slowly, gently, olive.

I touch my eyes
and glasses
with a Kleenex,
careful not to wipe
the holy light away.

THE TRAGEDIE OF Mac BEARD

for Bobby, who couldn't
read it then

Tousled (blond)
and sad-eyed (blue)
I wish he said
Mama I wish
that Daddy didn't grow
a beard.

It is the eye of childhood
fears the grey and prickly;
daddies should be smooth,
curly on head, and clean on chin.

The day I shaved it off
the black spikes floated
in the half-full sink:
will ne'er be clean.

He saw some blood,
patches of brighter scary red
against the new-scraped pink:
Mama he said does
Daddy's shaving hurt?
He dots blood on his face.

He watched the ritual
from soap to blade,
sideburn to jowl,
moustache to goat-like beard
to neck.

He never thought the old man
had so much blood in him.

I was sore, put corn starch
on my face (while he played
in the living room) from ear
to cheek, from nose to lip,
from chin to neck
and down.

Oh no he said
Daddy took off that
uzzer beard and now
he dots a white one.

Don't worry, son.
I'll never shake my snowy beard
at you. A little water
clears us of this deed.
Come here and help me wash.

Later he said he helped.
Mama he said I helped
clean Daddy's freckles
from the sink.

LETTER TO AN EDITOR

About your campus news scoop quote
more arrested for obscenity unquote
your spelling or typesetting really reeked.
You talked about a quote
four-letter world unquote
a quote obscene world
synonymous with sexual intercurse
unquote I wish
to praise you for your
judgment in unspelling
the offensive term quote
dash dash dash dash unquote
for if you'd spelled it
with your proven accuracy
some damn fools would be out
with signs quote
defend our right to use
the word quote
FORK unquote unquote.

YOU, ABCHIBALD MAC LEISH

"A poem should not mean,
 but be."

A poem, once it is,
should also mean,
make music, move.

FOR SALE

We saw
a tiny
tinny Christ
in cheap
gold plate
recrucified
among pink
artificial buds
inside a
clear glass
whiskey jug.
The outside said
NOT TO BE SOLD
OR USED AGAIN.

We didn't
check the price.
That has been fixed
almost two
thousand years.

BUT NEVER BY ME, CITIZEN

Adeline at Alcatraz
sounds like
a sentimental tale
in which a small girl
visits her convict dad.
It's not. It is
the shabby intersection
of two streets.

I park here,
locked and insular
and watch the flow
of Negro life.
I want to leave
the car, join
the flow, or think I do.

At midnight I am seen.
One tall broad Negro
looks, stops talking,
nudges others,
all turn toward me,
ready to approach,
the windows seem
like air, the car
no more than skin,
I turn the key,
tromp on the gas, and go.

I drive (sometimes)
through tunnels
half the night,
my rear-view mirror
shows me flashlights,
holding them are
tall broad Negroes,

back of them, pursuing me,
are other Negro men,
with dogs.
Always there's an end,
daylight, relief,
a "What was that about?"
Those are dreams.
This, tonight, is real.

———

I drive dark streets
beneath Caucasian lights
thinking of other nights
I tried, or wanted to:

The jazz place
in the spring
when Monk was there,
I drove past
at least three times,
but couldn't (somehow)
stop, park, go in,
unless I saw
another white man.
There were none.

The autumn night
a hitcher's roadside
white-toothed smile
leaped out of his
black face,
I drove off
(although I'd slowed
to pick him up)
telling myself
why I did, why
it was right.

Later, my hair black
on the pillow's pallor,
I drive again down Adeline
to where, at Alcatraz,
the crosswalk's white
leaps up from the asphalt.
The people are still
talking, waiting,
they've waited since
autumn, since spring.

I think I want
to face them,
say the truth:
"I like you, always
have, it's just (sometimes)
a drawing-back, a strangeness,
that I can't control."
At least that,
if I can't do more.

But I stay silent
in the car, the bed:
Unable to feel pride
at not having hated
nor done harm.
Secure from flashlights,
dogs, pursuit.
As guilty as the skin
I fill is white.

ELEGY IN PARENTHESES

The greengold Sunday
afternoon I heard
a horrified description
of the morning's accident
I knew she'd die.
The city was too far away,
a phone call meaningless:
I wrote an elegy.

(Some strange twilight intensity,
some not-yet-mourned-for,
Friday kind of look,
set her apart from all
the lovely, loved, and long-lived.
We should have known
that she would drown her autumn
while we danced our May.

An hour of grass and sun,
day to be young, to kiss
the air, caress the earth.
Death should have drizzled
from a cold grey sky
some day without a morning,
some week without a Sunday,
some year without a spring.)

Sometimes things make you wonder:
I wrote the elegy,
and then she didn't die.

NO MIRACLE

Things were bad.
Either we had to get away
or something in us
needed to get out,
like urine screaming
in our bladders.

So when you saw the light
start climbing there
behind the hill
I said maybe we're
the only ones can see it.
It was just the moon.
But as it climbed
it gave us both
this strong hermetic feeling
like being squeezed up
through a tube
till we'd pop out the top.

The moon rose with us
free from what had tried
to hold us down
whatever tried to stop us
doing what we had to do,
in the moon's case
get free and shine.

Our heads and shoulders
were protruding
from the tube
and we were moving up and out
when something
shoved us inside down
like counter-pressure
from two massive thumbs.

The moon got out, though,
stood big and round
and silver on the hill
and urinated light
all over us.

THE FLOWERS

" I want to be God, and therefore I try to change myself…
I look like him, only He has a calm gaze, and my eyes
look around me. I am a man of motion, not of immobility."
                                    - Nijinsky's Diary

There is a land
where flowers grow
in thick coiled clots,
as if you froze
the splash made
by a rockfall
in a pond
near-surface-thick
with yellow mud.

It is a land
of constant night
where cold slow
swirls of yellow
plaster the black sky
on cord-like stems
they do not need
to hold them up,
flowers always just born,
delivered by Caesarean
full-grown, each scar,
each stitch, each birth
mark starkly magnified.

Into that land Nijinsky
made his final leap,
then sat for years
immobile
learning to be God
by staring at the flowers.

LETTER TO DENNY ZEITLIN

The walls were glass,
dim light inside as out.
One vista: water, lights
and bridge just an extension
and expansion of the room.
Round white tables, orange
napkins, bay crests rippling
black and silver, tiny
bridge lights, street lights,
house lights, one great wink
of island light, a glow
of red to either side,
hillside houses, roads
with car lights glancing
off the glass as though
they'd drive into the bay.

But when you played,
our focus came in
toward your center.
The cosmos of your music
was our all.
Heads of the trio
moving with the music
set a rhythmic pattern
of their own. Feeling
of oneness: man
and instrument
and music; music,
instruments and men.

When you played, with just
the bass, those lovely
sounds called Quiet Now,
and then the drummer
brushed a whisper Shhh

across the night,
when you played your
solo cum concerto,
the others motionless,
heads reverently bowed,
when the gentle tapping
throb of folk theme
left no question
where it all would lead,
beauty was the word –
and gentleness; cathexis
was the word – and love.

And when you burst your
Carnival upon us,
we felt its moods
from light to grey,
sleepy awakening
to urgent frenzy,
slow lonely movements
to the churning throng.

It wasn't easy leaving:
You released us
to mundane tables,
parking lots, bridge
tolls and skyways
toward apartment beds.
We rode your music
almost all the way.

POEM FOR BERT LAHR

Your road
              of renovated yellow brick
is toll-free to pedestrians
but we still
              sit here on our butt
blaming our boots
for the faults of our feet.
Things have not changed
much here
              since yesterday.
You left, and left us
knowing we can't
              fill this hollow afternoon
with last night's laughter.

You never acted Lear
              (you wanted to)
but you were always
as much king as fool.

And we remember
your eyes well enough,
lighting that funny
              sad expressive
face that
       munched a thousand chips.
When you left
              we stood an hour
in clear dawn rain,
in barefoot sorrow.
Things haven't changed much.
Courage beckons, trembling,
              from its TV Oz
and Insight peers out
from its hovel on the heath,
where we have not played Lear

or even Lahr.
We're sitting here
            with one boot off,
eyes slightly raised.
And we'll be here tomorrow
unless God comes,
                      or Dorothy.

EPHPHETA

"And looking up to heaven, he sighed,
and said unto him, Ephpheta, that is,
be opened."   -- Mark 7:35

The cry of the peacock
was harsh. He huddled
in brown shadows
          with his mate.
And in his feathers
there were hidden
many eyes that wept.

But gorgeous is his
          plumage now:
A tail of copper-gold,
metallic green and blue;
majestic fan that spreads
and spreads, and fills
his iridescent house
with happy eyes.

SMALL BOY CRYING

A small Ohio
           village fair.
No stars above
           the ferris wheel's
gigantic up-and
           -over roll.
Empty seats on nearly
           all the children's rides.
Lights on the merry
           -go-round, a small
boy, blond beneath
           the lights, rides
all alone.
           In tears, he goes
round he goes
           up he goes down, his
broken heart
           riding around on
a big silver horse
round sadly
           up sadly down
as the music goes
           merry, and mocks.
Why does he make
           me feel as small
as he is,
           and as much alone?
How does he
           know that I'm
his father,
           that I'm watching him?
I have to find out
           who he is because
there are no stars
           above the ferris wheel.

FELINE NOCTURNE

A wise lean panther
paced the platform in the early evening
reading us the riddle of the Sphinx –
that lion-loined and cat-clawed
feline female

Outside we prowled
through sleek grey streets
our windshield wipers licking off
the cat tracks of the rain

Later two black tomcats
mewing pawed us at the bar
and at the microphone
a fiercely gentle jaguar
crouched to pounce
then sang, sprang
on his nubile prey

Toward morning we touched tongues
I touched your softest flesh and fur
my love-loined clawless kitten
and we purred

NOON: MARCH 13

Thru windowed
                pale sky sheen grey
                branches/warming
                sun play lilts
                my table
                As I watch light
                gliss
across and
    out
                to sparkle
            in the white
            that fell
            in last night's
                winter lightning
                a squirrel scrabbits
            past
        along a cable
                hi
        above the house

HAPPY

I get up much too late
for breakfast and the news
my students are undisciplined
and beautiful
rejection slips come
monthly from top magazines
my children act like kids
it's rained for twelve days
grass is long bright green
I haven't watched TV for weeks
the car needs four new tires
my sideburns are too long
to please the bowling team
and I've been sort of
happy lately

COLD SEPTEMBER NIGHT

Cold night
for September
twenty-eighth
Late to see
the green gleam
from a lighted pool
Coals glowing
in a smoky grill
Cold night
to be grilling
hot dogs or whatever
Scorch your front
and freeze your rump
Chilly even
taking bags of garbage
to the outdoor cans
Late bulb burning
in the neighbor's basement
Put the car
away already
Closed the door
of the garage
Cold and late
I'll put
a jacket on
and walk
beyond the pool
the grill the basement
to where that star
is shivering
above the corner
mailbox

SLEEPER

He's sleeping in his car
parked at the curb
head leaning hard
against the ridge
above the handle
of the door
Now every while a leaf
drifts drily by
and once and then a breeze
blows brittle leaves
along the driveway
skitter scratching
past the sidewalk
It's a stone-cool afternoon
November second and a saxophone
moans mellow from my stereo
He's snoring in his car
parked at the concrete curb

Four Poems For Jean,

who has done more
than understand

IF YOU WANT

So often
almost every night
as I turn over
face away from you
a habit started on our
first night, sleep time now,
so often
as I turn
I say the words
you've heard
so often
if you want
to hold me
touch me
        anything
at all,
I'm here
or if you want
to talk

NIGHT TOGETHER

You let me sleep
made three trips up
to see when I might
want to work
At last
you went to bed
yourself, and I
got up, and worked,
and here I am (two
minutes to two)
done with my papers
and my beer
I'm up with you
as much as you
were there with me
the hours I slept
Together doesn't
have to mean
we share a space
with bodies anymore
(You won't like "anymore"
and you'll be right
That wasn't ever it)
Let's sing
You there, me here
We're singing – what?
we know so many songs –
together
in the separated night

NEED

Night pain
wakes me
moaning your
hands reaching
knead me
I remember
nights of knotted
and unkneaded pain
lonely writhed
griped silent
bit back curses
rigid lay
til cramped calves
unclenched unclutched
as your hands
untense me
unknot me
calf smooth pain
soothed, removed

MARRY ME SOME NOW

Marry me some now / There are
so many ways and winds
this side of paradox
Wed me between alarm and dream
arresting morning / In chapeled evening
alter me with you
Blend us blindfold / drift on
white and warm
to (mid) night when the neighbors'
trees are tame
Blow high and sweet with me
and deep and sad / Come in my storm
as I come into yours
Who cares how many dawns and noons
we have been wife and man
Let's be again
Please marry me some now

WINDOW WINE

Candles burned
  rain
    splashed the windows
      while we ate

he got up
  the loved old man
    as if to pour
      wine in every glass

no one of us
  would take it
    but the dwarf
      he let
        the loved old man
          serve him –
          a dwarf

    "well when I
      get up / pour milk
      in mugs at noon
      I'm glad
      you take from me
      no one of you
      took wine tonight
      from loved old man
      I took
      so he would not
      feel sad"

on our cots
  night long we heard
    wine
      splash the windows
        in the dark

WORDS AND THINGS

I

You would think
wouldn't you
that I'd forget a few
but I remember
every   thing
and everything's
too much
to say in words

The first
I remembered
us saying
will have to stand
for all
although you
told me later
earlier words

You said   Now why
did you do that
and I said
I don't know
it just seemed right
We were always
big on words,
still are

II

I can't
but you've
forgotten much

I worry
what you've left

We weren't
unique but
even special
people aren't

We never
quite were one
but that we even
ungrammatically
were us
dies hard
with me

I'm tired
afraid
I'll say
this wrong
but
please don't
let us turn
at midnight
into a cliché

POSE OUT THERE

Pose out there
an inch beyond

my fingers

Don't let

me (ever) touch

Just let

me look
And I won't
(ever) tire of   you
I'll press my nose
against the wall
of air
and whimper
every time   you come
to let
me see   you

VISIT AFTER YEARS

Across your mind and room
this slender woman
                    walks
Small girls don't
play with baseball
                    gloves remember
She teaches now
in love with books
        and being young
Clock legs sprint
        around their track
She leaves / a little
                    tired
Between your hands
her father holds the warmth
                    she brought
Your thin grey love
limps out the door
        and follows her

OBJECTS

Your room
late afternoon
You've gone
A
piece of
chalk
not broken
on the
floor
bookmarks stiff
in paper
pages
opaque
windows greyed
stopped
shadows
I remove
myself
There are
too many
numb and lonely
objects in
your room
already

DOVE

for Bob Freeland

Dove, Arthur G.
Plant Forms (1915)!
Non-color Re
production:

soft grey nubs
of fuzzy snow
snub oval / hazy
fur ellipse

leaf feather edges
blur and blend / breast
billows overlapping
willow tips

bird murmurs
shadowed over
tones of
doveness

SEARCH NIGHT

Disheveled
into bars
where no one is
they want
to cars
whose children's
       sleepy eyes
        ask why
     to other bars
     with empty faces
     mirrors
           never find what
           they're afraid to
           whining how
           can she do this
           to us

           Momentary
           hands warm
       on each
   other's backs
     whose mouths kiss
    into mouth
an instant
words we're
good together
fingers clinging
to what's gone

SIX ON TWO

(These six parts may be shuffled and dealt again in
any order. The meaning should be different but equally
valid each time)

1   We're closer than we move

2   We let our silence talk

3   We know too
    much too little
    about us

4   We each try
    to play Sancho
    to the other's Don

5   What can be shared
    reflects what can be loved

6   We both must love
    what we can't ever share

NO SONGS BUT WHISPERS

This quiet morning
we've no wings
                but hands
July had wings
and flew where
we've no songs
                but whispers
mingling with the
after-midnight rain
and we're as new
as August
only deeper
somehow
we've no stars
                but eyes
and there is
nowhere we can
be
but here

PRESENCE

I.

What united
separates
what severs
joined
your there
is my then
is as here
as now
as we

II.

Two of us
were here alone
that night
the house
was crowded
I could not
attend

STAIN

Night slips
and cuts me
spurting warm
in summer's dark
Why turn
my life on
I'll see
nothing
flow away
but blood
nothing
cleanse
the dried guilt
staining
each knife
in my light

ARE YOU

Are you   Where
Someone in me
needs to know
Years passed
          you left behind
a girl I care for
She is not
          except in me
Where you are
for you too
          mourning is
          after known
     in nights
              of why
Where
If you answer
we will know
          you are

PARTNER

I think
I understand
What you do changes
What I do
You share my isolation
With you
I'm free to be alone
to
whisper lullabies
and walk on
fingertip
behind
your ear
and watch
your eyebrows
while you talk
and hold
your memory
like breath

BETWEEN US

Because your face
is never twice,
is always new

(Some shade of moon
soft crescents it,
some wisp of mood
tints   tilts)

I hold the warm known
fabric of your voice
up to the light

between your
unremembered lips
and my deft
listening eyes

PEACE

roar
         down reeling roads
past water   over
                     merging
       dark with flash
dark   horns   flash
turns confuse me   lose
      go to
come from
          a place of peace
          an empty
               fire escape
          with twenty
                    stairs to climb
                    a piece of
                    moon
               a book
          you said you
               wanted
               in my hand

SUMMER STORM

After the blocked black
      clouds
  and
      olive starts of rain
have whitened in our own
  base corners
After freedom hides
behind blown drizzle
behind the
    patches on the
      massed black pillows
After we have crept away
to silence
    no one else
has heard
  in the
safe   black   center
of the storm's one blood-shot
        eye
we will still
need a cause
outside ourselves

OF WORDS

We're built
      of words
in envelopes
addressed to us
we are
the stationary
love beneath
the moving words
we're why
the words
and what
we've written them
and made us

SWEET RAIN

Your music
frees / uncaverns ghosts
sad drifting things
thru fine
transparent rain
that tingles
buds / emerges blades
Your music
etches clear ghost-
lines of rain
from green sky
to grey grass
across my vastness

The Hour Before
The Wind

THE HOUR BEFORE THE WIND

In the hour

before the wind

when silence presses fingers

to the temples of our fear

nails   screws

                     bones loosen

seams and joints unglue

the six walls of this room

are thin as courage

dry as our mouths

and we are falling

              barometers

falling snow

as wind begins

                blows through us

in and out our windows

RUTH AND NAOMI

Ruth and Naomi
stood unbiblically
amid the sandy
soft confusion
of a county fair
and spoke of getting
married and begetting
children and the
dark tall one
asked the
short plump one
Do you wonder
what girlie
shows are like?
Will you go to
one with me?
and the other laughed
Whither thou goest
I will go
so they went
and satisfied
their curiosity.
One was my
college girlfriend,
married years ago
to someone else
and one my brother's
wife, who died
at thirty-three.
Their names were really
Ruth and Naomi.

ALTERNATIVE

Sad choice –

    with pregnant pity

nurse the walking

wounded I have maimed

or rush to tunnel in some

    womb of west or death

Love would give me an

alternative

inside unhappiness and guilt

a space

where I could live with

and because of

you

TWO FOR A BIRTHDAY

I. murmurings to you

I read the funny
                    cards
They weren't
I read the love
                    ones
They were too
            If you don't know
the way I feel
                by now
What have these
        strange sad years
            been all about

II. mutterings to me

Alone is
                always
        hollow, man
Don't sit there
        breathing
                        candle smoke
Gift-wrap
        your love
in case
        somebody
        ever wants it

BRIDGE TO SERENITY

Drive the sun
across
singing
and free
drop down
to green treed
parkways downhill
all the way
a valley
road surrounded by
immersed in peace

Now begin

I. Narrow stream
step rock
to rock
or   one clear leap
or barefoot
water up to
over knees
Log over
creek

Footbridge

    to enter park

       high

   high over

       gorge

II. Bridges are to cross

       NO PARKING AND

       NO U TURN

       ON THE BRIDGE

       To jump from

       is to rape

       a bridge

       to tear an

        ugly wound

      in its

        directioned flow

      But fear

           excitement

       parts of

crossing

SACRAMENT

Put your new

song in my mouth

I shall be

                wholly now

through you in

you with you

This   is

my   body

which your touch

makes ours

I've waited

    waited

to proclaim

your kindness at dawn

            your faithfulness

throughout the night

KAREN'S WORDS

I was
tiddly and
adorable

mistook
alliteration
for profundity

said to
Leslie
Fiedler

You are a much
misunderstood
maligned man

Yes
he said
I am

YOU HELP ME KNOW

Winter knows
          our need
          to be alone
melts away
I want
     so much
to give

you help
me know
we are
     each other's gift
we are

MIRROR

I've never asked before

was there a mirror

near the falls

next to the railing

where we stood

above the

plunging roar

and are you

looking in it now

here next to me

UNBROKEN

Now that you've read

my mouth   perused my hair

Now that you've freed

my fingers   raised me

still unbroken

from the crumbling stairs

Now that you've formally

presented me

handfuls of snow

Your salad bowl is empty

and my steak's a bone

Let's light

the cherries jubilee

DEEP

"the calcium snows of sleep"
- Stanley Kunitz

Dark is deep

less frightening

than white on white

as Melville knew awake

and Pollock

flecks of gold among snow

drifts bergs wastes

drop or rise to

pits of black deep

or night sky

look up

or down

the holes

that let dark in

are in the igloo ceiling

or the glacier floor

deep is no

direction

EXUBERANT

Some

phantom days

you flip

the door

a flirt

and Alice

Burglar

Toklas comes

    ballerining in

    in an orange

    sweatshirt

    and a ruthful

      grin

PERSON

Person
you are
where I start

I turned off lights
made streets invisible
        walls   sky
I made wrong
turns   lost
in white lanes
        sounds died
in lyric impulse
isolated in my
destination

Person
you are mine
and beautiful

I don't look
in a book
I make a step

Now my steps
fill your footprints
one by one
Behind me
steps you make
fill prints of mine

Person
you are
where I start

STAND BACK

I hold a lid
down on my dreams
I lifted my hand once
released the pressure
blew my arm off
now I hold it down
I wouldn't be
much good without
my other arm
but if you're
willing to embrace
an armless dreamer
all his life
stand back
I'll lift my left
hand from the lid

WILLING

I never wanted
to touch eyes before
to hold them
in my hand
but yours gleam
soft and brown
     and willing
     to be part of me
     just lend them
     to me while
     you sleep
I'll put your two
eyes in my pocket
carefully
and later I'll
reach in and touch
and feel
the way you see

TO HELP HER

He left the airport
just before the rain
to help her
start three mental
windmills turning
peacefully

He walked out
with his cello
in the middle
of the string quartet
to help her
drop three perfect pebbles
in symbolic streams

He stayed home
from the Forum
on the Ides of March
to help her
carve surrealistic
statues of her three
most recent dreams

He left her sleeping
in three rooms of wool
and memory and ran
across the fields
but turned back
at the snow fence
when he heard her call

WINTER CITY

(After reading some poems of Diane DiPrima)

Splinters in your hands
                Diane
from making fires
you ached till spring
to walk 10th Avenue
from 2 AM till dawn
and see no small cats
dying in the doorways

I don't know if you died
                Diane
or much about your
broken window floor bed world
the poet's grim room attic city
that you warned your
unborn child against
yet knew he'd see
enough to love
to break his unborn heart

Fifth Avenue at 2 AM's
cat-free
Up there my room's
so warm I'll open windows
The beds have mattresses
ten inches deep
                Diane
A parked cab's radio
is playing new sounds
by the Grateful Dead

CARPET

We sit in separate chairs

eyes memorizing our beginnings

feet touch the same soft

carpet   Part of it is how

your body last night

barely touching mine

flickers this mild room

with quiet lightning

THE WEIRD NEW BIRD

The weird new bird
will fly at sunrise
on her grotesque wings
above your clean blurred sand
across your green dim
pregnant hills soaring
with her own strange strength
her blacksword nose
bizarrely probing sky
her body poised ungainly
natural Watch her

SIMPLE

What you give me
is not
really silence
Minimal expression
sounds too fancy
but it's closer
and I'm closer
Here in your
near-silence
only here
I come to
beauty simply
Oh it's largely
love that makes it
simple
but it's
stillness too
as though you
washed me in it
hung me on
a line made of it
breathed on me
the simplest
beauty I
have known

ORDINATE

Burning velocity

in the presence

of quenching agents

is the ordinate

if presence

becomes absence

baby

SPECIAL BULLETIN

Huge air transport
smacks its neutral
belly on the border
roaring up in
orange anger
Warring rulers call
a hurried truce
to bury all survivors

MANDALAY MOONLITE

Three doors down's
an office where a little
man (lopsided face)
is leering at our pseudonym
and someone's watching goofy
Lucy one thin wall away
Our room's as bright
as Daylight Saving Time
and we're so warm
and kissed so curved
and stroked so Wow
do we feel good

CHANGES

"the spirit, measuring energy
in time and space. There is
nothing else to build from."
- James Waring

I

Begin with action

                aimless or extraneous

You may discover later why you did

Invent your field of action

Sense the boundless

                and dissolve the sacred limits

Your field keeps changing

and your action never is the same

Repeat it exactly in unbroken sequence

Study in depth and involve

Steer thru its changes

Get inside your action

and be

II

Attitude changes

                         not desire

Not frustration

                         attitude

Attitude

                         not consummation

Expression and the absence of it

push against each other

Feeling is suspended

and revitalized

                         between the two

The common/place is new

THREE DREAMS

Her dream: I'm dead
my women line mummed
corridors exchanging something
sad and questioning
her words he loved us all
the ways he could we can't
(we don't know how) only
share sorrow that he died

My dream: I'm too unpunished
too unchained I walk
in parks past sparkling lakes
and people
know I killed their children
and my sleeping friends
I murdered them
(I don't know how) it's hard
as steel to be alive

That other dream five years
away a continent ago:
remembered rooms my women
sleeping children in the dream
I grope from room to room
(I don't know how) goodnight
goodbye goodnight goodbye

INMATE

I stepped on sun squares
down white halls
to visit sterile
inmates
in starched rooms
I chattered condescendingly
above the soft foot dusk
Now I am stunned to see
barred window shadows
cross white stone
Stale sun motes now march
visitors to me
Dusk creeps
and Christ-crossed shadows
cover
impaled sterility

SINGS

steak and eggs

a shopping cart

    our first kiss home

a softly bursting bud

Odetta sang our bodies sang

    not sleepy and

there ain't no place

I'm goin'

wings and mouths

and nearly prayers

let's wash a little

have some coffee

    laugh

the afternoon still sings

BY PREFERENCE FROM ABOVE

Grope with froth
pale flesh lights
your fine blind antennae
down the slime slick
foot path you prefer
cross unseen water falls
still spilling in the
foaming black abyss

YOU NEVER DID

You never did
but I keep
seeing you
wade round that tiny
island of blueberries
naked legs cool feet
in water just below
your softly rounded ass
reaching smiling
                picking fingers
blue with juice
that trickles down
your slowly moving breasts

EMPTY

Do what's needed now
when emptiness is urgent
and essential anything
is in it and can happen
focus on the empty
sand ignore the rock
formations and relations
sand must have rocks
anywhere in order to be
empty never mind
the outcome do it now
and influence the past

AGON

Weapons drawn and raised and

drawn together irresistibly

two bristling close

antagonists

chins pushed in one

another's faces

Joined made one

their weapons

could be wings

SNOW

45 inches of

           Christmas Eve

snow in Vermont

I had visions of you imprisoned

for months you drove

your Volks out of Montpelier

determined on top of the snow

drove south on the Northway

then west thru the drifts

on the Thruway reached North

Drive before New Year's Eve

before Buffalo buried its head

in the drifts before I

was declared a disaster

EARLY

All those sad
late people
look at us
on-time ones
as if we
forgot to wipe
don't even
mention being
early

WHAT COLOR

the handyman
for many reasons
I dislike the term
a friendly middle
aged black man
is moving cans
and cleaning
in the cellar
and I'm sitting here
thinking of Bob
Lanier who just signed
for a million
and a half
and all the white
fans who are glad
he got it hope he
buys a big house
in a nice black
neighborhood
remembering a white
child's questions
what color is my face
what color are my
eyes what color are
my friends

A VERY GOOD WAY

A very good way
your head on my chest
flesh blessing us
wind not entering
our blankets
a voice I recognize
as mine
or maybe yours
repeating words
we used to need

INSTRUCTIONS

repeat

repeat

repeat

repeat

Break Through

NOW A MOTHER

the laughing quiet happy one
was you those summer nights
of gin badminton lobster drive-ins
serious and gentle talks at tables
driving through snow-rutted streets
as dusk fell on the mothers houses
children we both loved
as much as I have hurt
you understood more than you're humble
sure you don't have answers
everyone's too sure he has
and now a mother you
it's beautiful it's right it
fits

STILL

I passed the drugstore
with the clock today
The phone booth wasn't
being used It still
seems strange to drive
past when it's empty
It looked warm this
afternoon and what
an ice-case it was
seven months a year
The clock-face is still
lighted nights I thought
you'd want to know
and light or dark it's
still ten minutes
until three

WAYS WE USE IT

The guilt of memory
the ways we use it
walking flat stones
skipping every other wave
swimming with old
bodies in new seas
burying our eyes in sand
climbing into depths of grasses
tops of hills where once
we lay at picnics
in fields high with memory

NIGHT

The curve of you
warming along me
my bourbon body/ache
creeps toward your healing
The tense night
walks a taut wire
into dawn Your salt
tears dry forgiving
Your fingers
ease the tightness
in my groin

COME BACK

You left
the door open
I waved twice
Dark doesn't fall
things just get
less distinct
Come back
why don't you

CHAIR

1

Look up
and see a yellow shape
Say chair
But you see
just the yellow shape

2

Mind might not jump
to chair
Might think of
color beauty form

3

Tired you'd
pass from seeing
into sitting
Thought
emotion
use
Your dog would
have jumped quickly
on the chair

FIRST BASEMAN

1

Mel's a limping legend
always gets the most
applause
Left leg a crippled
stick of flesh
he plays first base
If he had two good legs
he'd make the major leagues
No lucky hits   he has to
drive the ball to have time
to limp to first
Broad shoulders   chest
thick body
on a heavy strong
right leg   thin
spindle of a left

2

He'd hit home runs
in any other park
but here no fence
the fielders chase the ball
to hell and gone
and throw it back
He hit one home run once
the ball went up and out
and sailed on far across
the fielder's head
Mel sweated base
to base to base
skinny leg in back
big one in front
he shuffle gimped along
struggling slowly
all the way around
we bathed him in applause

3

Tough place to play
first base   the ball
if it gets past you
rolls for half a mile
Mel couldn't chase it
never lets it past
Grotesque and beautiful
he plants that stick
of left leg on the bag
turns stretches
he grows taller
arm gets longer
big glove reaches clear
across the diamond
catches everything they throw

4

Should be in the stands
his beer-gut broader
bald spot bigger every year
have the decency
to keep his bad leg
out of public view
But Mel's at first base
Sunday afternoons
his thin leg on the bag
his hefty body twisting
sweating snagging
infield throws
or leaning at the plate
magnificent and awkward
His strong arms whip
the bat around
to smack the ball
out where the fielder
is still chasing it
We all cheer wildly
as he drags his limp
to a stop at first   Applause
like Yankee Stadium

and then a sudden

hole of silence

in the very center

of the cheering

as someone with two legs

comes in to run

for Mel

BURN DARKLY

look lonely
shadows look with you
flutes heard
across brown carpeting

burn darkly
by yourself
the sharper loneliness
cuts thru

melody so strong
you lose it
if you
lay it on too hard
be a guitar
absorbing dark
releasing soft
deep song

LOVING QUIETLY

Loving quietly
this morning
not to wake
        their children
playing quietly
this afternoon
not to wake
        their father
working the long night
returns at dawn
children asleep
their mother turns
returns
their father's touches
loving waking quietly
        each other

UNIMPORTANT

Things we don't do
              unimportant reasons
day it didn't rain
sun coughing in the trees
put the grill away had
dinner in the living room
roof between us and
the rain that didn't fall
door stood open all that
rainless evening
we looked out and wished
we'd been as open

DOWN 89

I drive in dark down 89
sweat angry from a hundred miles
windshield bug-squished
headlights glare
I blow my nose   blood
spreads thru kleenex to my hand
some small live thing
hits my back wheel
a sick dead thump
I'm past before I see you wave
drive miles to turn around
curse screech to stop for you

off 89 in spruce row camp
blind naked writhing
in a rented lean-to
I bleed on both of us
the sticky spread of sick
frustration in the dark

turn me on my back
kiss blood away
make love sufficient
midnight bearable
this paid shack
a kind of home
let these be our suburbs
grasses streams
and branches breathing
near our sleeping bag

CLEAN

The rain is clean and quick tonight

to run in

cold and streaky

on my back and legs

and soaking my long hair

the way it falls

and fills the silence

till it overflows

ZOO

Across a fence and moat
a polar cub named Zero
prounces down and up
within his mother's
polar gaze   Behind some
iron bars a mini-monkey
sucks his mother monkey's
teat then clings to her
cage-climbing tummy
her ring-running back
A metal plaque beneath
the hunting cissa's cage
says in captivity
the coloration of this
wild bird fades
from blue to green

TIMES LIKE THIS

A night much warmer
than I guessed not
many people pass
a few stars barely visible
among the last leaves
lower man-lit stars
a cluster of them
near the bridge
below the iron rails
move off around
a greentree curve
in friendly light
a dog's bark no more
hostile than a tree's
but I walk back
the way I came
So many people die
each night so many live
are born unwanted
there must be places
times like this
a world can hide
its troubles on
the bridge of the
electric stars
my feet plough leaves
brown trodden but not
wet or dirty on the
sidewalk just one cardboard
from one beer six-pack
goes in a garbage can

I came out walking troubled
looking to find more
I'm glad now I forgot
my key on purpose I can
knock and let you
let me in

LETTER

This letter
    from your father
    came today
about us
I wanted very much
    to open
    rain is falling
    I have dinner
almost ready
ten more minutes
    I can drive to you
    hand you the letter
read it to me
driving home
    look I brought
    your father's letter
    dry unopened
in the car
beside me thru the rain

JIMI

–

The thunder's over
and the rain begins
pocking the silence
with a brutal brief
September hail
Your axe hit hard
            it's broken
and amputated birds
bleed black on free ways
where speed reigns
reins in lost flyers
mourning for their wings

–

The rumor clung for months
you'd 'shot your
brain'   you 'were a vegetable'
      then
there you were at Woodstock
wiping people out
with Purple Haze

We'd just got used
to knowing you were
really there   or here
when you outshot the rumor
in a blazing duel
high as noon

—

Your music still screams
from cassettes
                turntables
flicks man
but you're dead
they've buried your
wild Afro and your
                slashing axe
The hail was brief
but hard
The thunder's over
and the rain
falls senselessly

QUESTIONS FOR JANIS JOPLIN

'don't believe
that things get
better just stay stoned'

How high is hell

do you climb to it

thru your own pierced

sockets thru the

blinding needle's

lonely eye

singing blue and

stoned gets harder

do you climb

blood ladders

spiderwebs of veins

do scarred arms

reach to pull you

up to hell

do things get

better there

PEACE SIGN

Main Street traffic
5 o'clock
I'm driving carefully
YOU'RE THE WORST
DAMN DRIVER
I look around
no way that livid
screamer could mean me
DRIVERS LIKE YOU
he means me all right
KILL MORE PEOPLE
THAN WARS
I blink three times
and start to understand
AND GET THAT
PEACE SIGN OFF
YOUR FOREIGN CAR
YOU S.O.B

VOICE

This poem's
for a voice once
on a telephone
at 2 A.M.
that told me
my last dime
had dialed
a wrong number

COOLLY

Here we sit in billiard-green
cloth lawn chairs
on our exclusive hill
applauding our team in the battle
'raging' way down there
our boys our insects
winning cleanly over *them*
Here we sit   our hair
just grey enough
but too long for our age
coolly calling marijuana grass
as well as creeping bent
One had thought battles
as a social spectacle
went out with Tolstoi
but we raise our stemmed martinis
in a toast to this
most recent late late show
It's raining down there
we remark   too stormy now
to see much
war called because of darkness
On our hill
each stemmed glass
holds an eye
that was an olive
each eye looks upward
to the still bright skies
where Someone clad
in our team's raiment
walks by triumphantly
beneath his halo helmet
like John Wayne

EPITHALAMION

We two know a little
about love
how the cup keeps filling
as it overflows
how love must be
the blown snow
between dark trees
whenever it is not
the trees themselves
how bells could never sound
or water taste the same
once we had heard
and tasted them together
We know that love
is built of sorrow
care   respect   and joy
we know that
flowers rise and turn
leaves turn and fall
snow falls and melts
into the sunlight
We have much more to learn
we vow today our willingness
to learn it all   the poverty
the poetry   the pain
the ever filling
always overflowing cup
the sound of water
and the taste of bells
the winter woods
We vow now always
we will share
a name   a faith   a home
an ever deeper love

GIVE

receive is give
we overflow
I miss what
you won't have
because of me
although not get
is also give

PROMISE NOT TO

with only hands
I give her
promise not to
lose or send away
after I am left
she must continue
although all of
everything has changed

WALKED

If I walk back as if
I'd never crept away
knowing you're there
dark but not asleep
you'll tell me how
things overtake us
wasting time you
always thought I'd
come   then your
voice will cease
your sheets will still
be clean and cold
you'll realize
I've changed my life
you won't question
so hard you won't
comprehend   you will
still breathe my
fulfillment   feel
the grave pulse of
my joy when I've
walked away to
where I am

SOMEONE

I need you and I'll wait
but I can't quite remember you
I think I met you
on the eve of someone's death
I'd like to go see him tonight
but it's so snowy
I might miss his house
I'll wait and I
suppose you'll come
I'd like to be with him
but I can't walk that far
                and back
and it's too cold
to spend the night there

CHARLES BURCHFIELD: ORION IN WINTER

Midnight midwinter
earth and sky
are stars and frost
Sir you designed
the sky to bring
the constellations close
and real
and set the whole
white universe in motion
made frosted earth
in five days less
than God
and wrote the sky
new winter's tales
the stars your
rhythms crossing creasing
skies of yours   the restless
spirits of the breaking
winter stars cold fires
hard frozen leaps of blue
—white flame   Orion and
Orion and Orion
icy stars are
sticking to our eyes
icicling down our spines
down your raw white
tall rock of earth
beneath your wheeling
world of sky

POEM FOR JIM SULLIVAN

I don't know what some words and letters
mean Words like leukemia and course and
required On New Year's Eve you showed up
at my door coat full of snow big smile (you
always smiled) and the paper you had written
for my course You wanted to do all that was
required You did and got a B By then I knew
you had leukemia and went to Roswell once
a week for treatment and that you'd soon
be staying there a week or more I didn't know
that now in early March a principal on the P.A.
would say on Wednesday morning that you'd died
I don't know what some words and letters mean

OK

There are so few of us
Before the curtain rises
fewer   What if you
and I are left
to face the faces
What if everybody's
in the audience but us
and knows it's real
What if our tongues
and bodies say the
things they say alone
the things we dream
It's OK isn't it
I took so long to know
it's OK if the world
walks in and watches

NEED

we need a meeting place not these

walls of transparent photographs

and records playing soundlessly

glass lovers looking listening

we need to really feel

before our memories

are bundled like old papers

in a basement corner

NEW BEACH

Lake Erie islanded in ice
the driftwood white sand
warm this April
this is our new beach
to doze and campfire on
to burn a little
of the beautiful white wood
and walk along the sunset
to our last year's beach
the ice black velvet patches
on the lilac sky-lake
two miles north along
the skyway stacks
puke smoke on Lackawanna

EPITAPH?

is it

enough

an epitaph

he cared

ISLESBORO

visitors and summer

people swarm less here

some rock-jut sense

of permanence

the ferry leaves something

returns to something real

gulls

fly through the glass

throat of Dark Harbor

and line up along a roof-spine

wild roses

foliate a bush-edged

beach of pebbled shells

slim birch trunks whiten

clouds surround

themselves with sky

blue water glides beneath

sailboats and lobsterpots

the white mailboxes nearly

all are stenciled Pendleton

the other year-round

residents: Penobscot Bay

and silence

RELATIONSHIP

We can't stay strangers
and we're not yet friends
In this new larger house
your mother shares my
father's bed and name
but they are out somewhere
tonight and you are not
my brother he is in another room
and I am not your sister
she is with him they are
strangers talking trying to be
friends and they seem far away
and younger than the hungry way
my mouth accepts your eager tongue

I'M EARLIER

I'm earlier.
Your nose above
my blanket knows
you're warm as I
was not too sorry
for my cold
floor toilet feet.
I'm earlier now
mornings toddling
from clock to
ringing faucets. Half
asleep means half
awake. Snow blows
thru blinds and drifts
across the phone.
Deodorant sprays my
cold breath against
the glass. I snuggle
back some measured
minutes. My nose in
your blanket knows
I'm earlier.

REACH NEAR

Arms and fingers flicker
over others' shoulders
in dark tents of stroking hair
where flesh is fabric
cloth is skin
closeness smolders in whose
loving fingers feeling whose
loved foreheads noses chins
to touch is to be touched
I touch myself barely aware
I warm myself   warm whoever's
legs and backs are close
Reach near   touch warmth
of hair and flesh-filled clothing
everywhere   no need to think
move gently loving arms
and chests warm palms
and feet   hands moving down
the backs of legs and
fingers tracing new-known faces

Suicide Prevention Center

1

Ignoring other phones
we've talked two hours
tears dry his throat
resigns "I'm gonna
put the phone down now
I hafta cut my wrists again"

twelve times before

I speak his name
the phone cord bleeds
across the desk-top
down the floor
I know he will
emergency knows his
address too well

phones ring I listen
to a troubled kid
whose parents don't
like his long hair

2

The floor relaxes between calls
the walls breathe easier
spoons stirring laughter
into coffee almost melt
it's been a long shift
heavy calls   the chairs are
swaybacked from the five
hour ride   we pounce on
MAY I HELP YOU   a
wrong number   wow imagine
getting this place by mistake
we laugh more than the joke
deserves   a phone rings
and like firemen or like
fighters we respond and
May I Help You

3

ATTICA

You read it in the paper
didn' you   nobody tell me
if he dead   my man
in Cell Block D
don' know if I kin stan' not
knowin'   he no bad man
took some money f'om a
liquor store to feed us with
but he don' hurt no one
he b'lieve in Doctor King
an' God an' now they killin'
forty men down there
don' know if I kin stan' this
waitin'   pray for
ever'body's man black man
or white   I tol' my man
jus' always to be peaceful
do what guards an' warden want
an' now they shoot an' kill
don' know if I kin stan' not
knowin'

4

Your pain opens like
a body and I enter
our two voices make
love half the night
sorrow washes back
and forth in words
and silence   we repeat
we listen and you're
lifted in the
climax of your grief
our voices part
like combed hair
and we're each alone
I slowly pull out
of your pain and feel
mine draw its skin
again around me

5

Tape calls   log tapes

describe   dispose

schedule   register

fill every form

each line   all items

carefully

and this means me

there is a troubled

human right behind that

tape recorder just beneath

that pile of forms

crying through that phone

I came to help him

move those mountains

off the desk and

let me try

6
MARY

no one listens any one

                    don't care

tunnel through that mound

of sleeping pills to morning

stop that night thing screaming

                    in my ears

it fangs my eyes they're sore

please listen some one

it's cold hell alone

floor full of rusting blades

and broken glass and bleeding

ice   oh never mind no body

has to ever listen any more

my words are strong and wise
as winter travelers   their bread
and voices frozen   their eyes
closed to light   my words
were children   they are ghosts
they will be windows in a storm
they will be shattered blindly
scattered glass confetti
blown torn words

8

Thanks for letting me out man
I hope you have a good night
now plunge into Main Street
midnight walking like
a half-drunk derelict
spewed out here by a
clock's unfeeling mercy
lighted windows on the
fourth floor where my
friends are answering the
phones I might stop hearing
later in my sleep   should
quit it takes too long
to scrape me off the ceiling
every time I'll go back
though I'm hooked on helping

STILL LIFE: DECEMBER

So there's a tall red
                    standing candle
and a shorter green one
and there's a Scotch
                    pine branch
long-needled next to them
an even subtler color than
                    the candle-green
and something gets to me
and I pull out one-dollar
bills (three – all I have)
and put them greenside up
down on the table
The sick thing is that their
green's fresher than the
                    branch and candle
and looking at the Scotch
pine needles I think many
and looking at the candles
                    I think two
and looking at the dollars
I read one   one   one
and George lies there on his
three faces in the candle-
melt and needle-
                    fall

DREAM

I walk stubbornly
into your mirror
bounce once
then crash glass
across your plush
white carpet
let my cut fore arm
bleed dot-drip-dash
into your dining room
wobble backward and
die exactly in the
middle of your
living room

ONE MORE WAY

I've said I'm sorry
all the other ways I know
sound hollow in my heart's
                              throat
like all the sadly true clichés
this hurts you more than I
always hurt the one I love
in these defenseless hours
before day light when night's
a wet black vast and sky
cries soft black stars
down on our mourning sleep

RE-RUN

Afternoon
after night
you're stunned still
carrying our quarrel
like an unborn child
I've worked away
        and back
to where you're
clenched around it
We can pour soft liquor
on the rocks of sorrow
we can watch this
        re-run end
Man: how can you use
my love this way
        Woman: how
can you use my pain

THAW

rain is wetter and more silent now
last fall it thrummed on roofs
and swirgled down
      the gutters floating leaves
now it falls in greyish snow
brings dim false hopes of spring
of people blanketed on grass
content within their bodies
eyelids brushing tiny rainbows
raindreams better than this
         soggy thaw

WORDS FOR GARY

Loving you was at least
as hard as loving
my father but for very
different reasons
With you the kind of love
was new was what
I'd never quite been
sure was right to feel
Love for my father
was expected natural
and eminently right I
couldn't feel it that
was all I love you both
now in the ways you
want me to whatever
that means and is worth
It's easy now and maybe
that's why I keep
asking why it wasn't
easy when it mattered most
I said a lot of it once in
a poem to the woman who came
between in ways she couldn't
know and we could not
do much about I guess
the same was true once
of my mother a son and
husband both in love with
her the son believed
himself so much more sensitive
and capable of feeling love
when it was only in the
showing that we differed

THE NEW YEAR'S POEM
ABOUT DIANA

If you knew her
you don't know she's dead
You've all picked up a phone
to call her
or addressed her
Christmas card
or driven your car toward
her house
or you've waved
walking by the library
But those things
wouldn't be unusual
Death does take getting used to
They're not the things I mean

You still go to her for advice
                    and get it
move close to her for warmth
                    and feel it
reach out to her for love
                    receive it
come to her in...
I started to write 'prayer'
and stopped
her fingers pressed my right wrist 'no'
but all of you believe in her
Faith is a door marked 'Friend'
you enter
and begin another year

JANUARY: BERRYMAN

"The high ones die, die. They die. You look up
and who's there?
- Easy, easy, Mr. Bones. I is on your side.
I smell your grief.
- I sent my grief away. I cannot care
forever. With them all again & again I died
and cried, and I have to live."

- Henry

So John went somewhere, following his grief,
coughing his proper blood, his fingers
dusting fading worlds, his worlds unhanding him,
pulling up bearded roots, exposed like bones,
and washing pills with gin.

He wrote love songs across two centuries.
His head, heart overflows.
He writes about the burning blinds
between what he can see and be,
the friendly ground where he could never
rest and be bored to/by death.

He came to praise, man, not to bury
but every high one that he knows was damned
Blackmur   Delmore   Faulkner   Plath
Williams   Stevens   Roethke   Frost
Henry   Delmore   Randall   Bones

He goes to pieces, finally,
wrote himself into a corner of a room
near an open window with a river view.
So it was frozen white and my God cold.
It wasn't dark, and then it is.

EVENING EVERYTHING

My eyes weary
holding up this white
hillside,
        strain lifting
that black railroad bridge
to make it touch the lemon-
silver weight of sky.
I fly awake
        to you appearing
in the clean fierce air
up there where even I
know you can't be.
But even garbage
        frozen into
several hill-foot ponds
is glazed pale yellow,
evening everything.

INDIAN DOOR

I need a door the color
doesn't matter or the lock
I'll leave it open anyway
I'm not sure what doors mean to you
A stranger opens most doors
in answer to our knock
steps aside stiff
to let us pass and
closes them again
A door fell on you once
someone removed the screws
that held the hinges held
the door in place it fell
on you Remember every
detail of your life and know
things could have been
much better or much worse
Are you afraid of doors

I hear some great great grand
grandfather tell his son
An arrow missed me and I
ran straight for the door
I knew the Indian was in
the woods and coming I was
frozen crazy I remembered every
detail of my life then leaves
blew down the steps and in
and then that Indian with
snarling silver in his teeth
This wasn't what we'd aimed at
these slaughter scenes not what
we'd toiled for and looked
forward to He came out of
the woods and through the door
and grabbed me by the hair and

threw me back I knew I'd killed his
family This thing of darkness
I acknowledged mine He lifted up
his knife and I knew how to die
I knew how he would take my scalp
it was the last I knew except
somehow I lived Things could
have been much better or much worse

We need a door to open friendly
without stiffness let the leaves
blow down the steps and in

We need an Indian to enter
smiling silver right behind
the blowing leaves We need
a door the color doesn't matter
or the lock We'll leave it
open anyway

SOMEWHERE NEAR DAWN

I

No strength no words no anger left
we trudge toward snow-filled sleep
along two separating trails
into two different darks
But must I cross alone
this great flat field
of greying guilt this field
in greener seasons intimate familiar
become so bare so unprotected
hands inside my gloves numb
seeing through these leafless bushes
those blank fields beyond despair
my feet aching cold turn
back and I begin to run
breathing thin air through
stiff-haired nostrils
puffing weary clouds of steam
I see you running toward me
through the heavy snow all our
four feet tramping to
get warm get home

II

We meet somewhere near dawn
where birds return to spring
a magic sky flies round us
melting fear and dark away
through breathing doors through
warming corridors of spring
light gracious swallows
carry my soft urgencies
we talk with fingertips on
shoulders faces two mouths breathe
on ice-glazed panes until one
warm round hole is melted through
and we can see the great flat
field outside can almost see
the frozen footprints lonely
sleepers left last night
trudging through snow so sad
so grey so deep it seemed
it couldn't ever end

COLORS

In the mall parking lot
these two girls held
        the elevator door
so I could help you limp on in
they smiled in sympathy
at bare toes pinking
        from your cast
we all admitted "we don't know
what floor to get off on"
"we have to wait and see
what color it is" one girl said
the floor where they got off
        was yellow

ours was green
it was nice to joke
about their color being
different from ours
and none of us
        got hung up
they were black or
we were white

LINE

The drizzled line for tickets
turns the corner
        in the blurring rain
it lifts and forward drops
its heavy feet and stands
where red wet letters say no
standing here to corner
Nearby all its children wait
in warm dry cars
Its raincoats hang inside
rooms closed like cold wet fists
rooms dry as memory's umbrellas
It's wool-wet it's pavement-tired
determined to obtain
pneumonia's worth of
        circus for its kids

SENTENCES

ONE:

      The empathetic judge was kidnapped by your
lawyers late last night at your request. Now wipe
the perspiration off your conscience, and absorb
the stare of twenty-four impartial eyes.

TWO:

      You hid your madness well, but must have
known we'd find it sometime. You were clever
packing some of it between the petals of this daisy,
tucking some behind this barmaid's eyes, and scattering
the rest like gravel all across this ocean floor.
Your case will be remembered and discussed.

THREE:

      You, Artist: You shall breathe the charged
air of each present moment, wash in the foaming
rapids of reality, walk on the knifeblade edge of
life until you die.

BARS

She played guitar
and sang down there
and we sat high and
watched her through the bars
Bars everywhere on railings
windows walls the radiators
looked like bars even guitar strings
finally and she was nervous
it felt like performing
and she wanted us to share
a stairway window
well and balcony
It should have been much free-er
than the formal room we'd left
but even music warm with
laughter couldn't loosen us
when all those bars were there

CLING

A door was not
even closed
A mother (a
ghost) went
an other way to
some inner where
Left here on a
haunted stairway
a daughter clings
to a father
knowing behind him
is an outer door
about to be opened

I'M ALMOST AWAKE

I'm almost awake
I know
but just before
there's this partition
to slide open softly
closet I must tiptoe into
sleeping one to touch goodbye to
with these sentimental fingers
which remember
after I'm awake

WHY

Why are we swept down sudden angry streams

past unknown islands

          where familiar branches

               brush our hands

Why must we know the urgency

               of rapids

     and the fear of rocks

see awesome spuming whiteness

at the edge of

        falls

before we trust our instincts

reach out   save us

clinging to each other

       in the crazy rush

ESSENCES

(for Jennifer, before
her first birthday)

"Watching" you, my smallest neighbor, I

let you play along the fence and toddle

toward this reddest rose. Your fresh

new eyes see Rose breathe, open. It's im-

perceptible to me; I barely guide

your chubby hand past thorns. Your

fingers touch one petal, smooth between

eager tips: hold, press, caress: feel

deep in petal some soft flow I miss.

You kiss it, to your tongue's delight:

find three clear flavors: Silky, Delicate

and Red; I don't. You will forget, I guess,

who let you near; but not the *rose.* Eyes

will remember, fingers will (that little

while), and tongue. As soon as you can talk –

I need words, Jennifer – please teach your

tallest neighbor how to see, and feel; and

teach me how to taste these essences again.

WISH

for a voice named dō dē

When you talk to your self

as you talk to me now

but in that crowded lecture hall

observed by "them"

I wish that I could be there with you

could focus on the left (left!) nostril

of your "evil" face

could hear the voice I'm hearing now

as clear and sad as Sonny Fortune's flute

could hold your voice

and you

one tiny instant

balanced on the palm of my left hand

THINGS THAT MATTER

This heavy summer
thick with humid
memories No time
or energy for
things that matter
Sweat getting mixed
with every thing
Your letter let me
breathe cool air
I thought it would
be cool to see you

SANE PERSON

Walk with grace: the times are evil
Stand up straight: nothing of use is left
Swim in the dew: become relentless
Recall life's color: family comfort,
    the need to try your talents on a
    wider stage, the old life-colored
    bathrobe that your mother put on sick,
    degrees that you obtained and tucked away
Remember sitting in your mother's arms
    as dark trees sucked a sound from wind,
    as your child-eyes sucked light from fire,
    as doors you opened rivaled stars with
    inner light, as rocks were only hard
    compared to human skin
Whisper something holy they can quote above
    your grave, make ends a means to better means
Sane person: stay away from all locked wards

SORT OF WANTED

I dialed and
you answered and
I said something dumb
about a call I didn't
want to get so I
was keeping the
phone busy calling you
I almost got the
truth out later though
I said I sort of
wanted just
to talk to you and
even   uh
apologized for what I'd
called the reason
for the call
said it had been
my 'immediate excuse'
Our talk was short
and tentative
but I liked it a lot
and had a kind of
feeling you did too

WEAK

We who are weak

think always every

other one is strong

lash with our

weakling weapons

anger   sarcasm

sometimes destroy

the weak we

saw as strong

destroying us

LAST

When you meet a Danish friend say "Tak
for sidst" which means "Thanks for the
last time we were together." The thank-
ingest people in the world have a "Tak"
for everything. So "Tak Birger Christ-
ensen" for the most enviable furs ever.
-- ad in *New Yorker*

You are not Danish and
do not own furs and
the ad does not mean *last*
of course but latest or most
recent Anyway I don't think
I pronounce right "tak for
sidst" and I don't have a
tak for anything and last
for us means sadly simply
last
     and I'm a thanking
person but being clear
is always hard as hell for
me – strange parallel: is
hell hard? – and all the
sad songs ever written are
about us now and they all
say we shall not ever
meet again
so now it should be safe
to say without trans-
lation Thanks
for the last time
we were together

Warm Brooms

This book
is for
my mother
Anna Keller

AS NAKED AS THE ROOM

As naked as the room

we sit on floors warm

brooms have swept

and say words there's

no need to clothe

In this stripped place

our hearts remove their veils

Nude fingers meet

along a broom straw

and our warm question's

answered now but never asked

OPEN

Shell

cracked

exposes

Softness

torn

opens to

softness

encloses

QUIETLY

your

body

spoke

my

name

and

swam

to

me

I

too

don't know

where all the

love

came from

SLOWLY

for Kathy

Learn slowly
how to want
The reassuring light beside the bed
    goes out
you reach for someone
    gone
your dreams
    are strangled
    by the jangling clock
morning's to be born

Learn slowly
what to need
A way of knowing
    any nose
      is beautiful
    handfuls of melting snow
      are precious gifts
    those strange familiar hands
    caressing what you love
      are yours

PLACE

My roots

are in my soul

A place is good

worth living in

love's there

if I reach

out for you

and I keep

finding us

DANCE

You know

how I

my feet

don't dance

        but

I would

love to

move with

loving

you and

you can

call it

dancing

if you

like

SELF

A clear

drop glides

its branch

inside its

tube of ice

survives

makes its

own warm

its self

worth being

LEAVING

All morning it's been

rain and pretty cold

(That night the rain

will enter all my rooms)

Now almost noon

we'll meet in one

of our warm places

for an hour

A white-branched

birch across the street

not leaving yet

looks clean as winter

cold as distance

CALL IT WISDOM

"Pain comes from the darkness
and we call it wisdom. It is pain."
                              -Randall Jarrell

Dream
        of the end
of anything
Hurt now
you hurt forever
I see you
        as you are
and pour
my unkind gift
into the porches
of your sleep
The pain
        you wake to
will not be
like mine

OUR WORDS

To be with me

say them slowly

      Really

not so hard

now is it

Say them

      Kiss our distance

lightly with each one

Each one

a way

FIVE SONGS

SONG #1

Some part of us is always being new
No road unrolls before us or behind
No time is measured on our patient clock
The world is built on emptiness
A knowledge that will never make me wise
I wake in dark   Can't move my hand
It always makes me sad
Not fear   I can't recall the dreams
We make love in the soft pale light
Some part of us is always being new

SONG #2

Miles between unreal
no feeling of apart
We came together
    breathless
in our oneness
shattered in a
                thousand
                        tiny
yet still strong
and love and one
Eyelids wet with
joy and wonder
want me want you
Unreal miles between

SONG #3

cannot be written down
all lovers sing it
and they'll understand

SONG #4

Still August
Brittle leaves blown brown
down past the grey
stone railing

May mad with green
Rain springing trees buds
things from branch and earth
June rain but not to wet
sun-torched July's scorched
grass the sprinklers cross

Leaf drops leaf
drifts and settles
restless near the grey
stone stairway
still still August

SONG #5

Dive alone
where I can't
reach or follow
We can't be
         each other
Depth is lonely clear
You're sad for you
and all the world
You'll rise from sorrow
slowly swimming strongly
someone longer strangely purer
I can't join you
         or deprive you
Dive alone

SEARCH

for Barbie

Daddy do you go to search

You meant church

but search was right love

right and hard

rejecting if and finding yes

a strange ascent without

a lonely omen or a flight of birds

to this bare hilltop

with no weapons against friends

On this rock I build my search love

Shall I name it after you

LOOK IN HIS FACE

Look in his face
him over there
flow in and out
of it somehow
don't try to tell me
what he's thinking
or what kind of room
he goes to nights
don't try to build a bridge
from what you know
to what you see
his face may hold
the past new as a pink
unpricked balloon
now needs resuscitation
mouth-to-mouth
don't ask what bed
he's been in last
don't listen to him lie
look in his
face and
don't be so
afraid you'll understand

5 years before we met
I saw Demuth's *I Saw
the Figure 5 in Gold*
from William's *The
Great Figure* where 5's on
a fire truck thru the city
then we both saw 5 the
          Indiana postcard
Creeley sent and we read 5
a Numbers poem now in
Creeley's *Pieces* book
since we bought these
numbered glasses Twin
Fair discount store you've
always let me drink from
number 5

I WINCE AT

I wince at

not limbs nailed

to wood crossed beams

but eyes pried

out vile eyes

of pride too

fierce to feel

POEM FOR MY MOTHER

vast silence scatters

dark star seed

conceives so many

tiny buds of light

rains with such care

past petals

past each star

to reach me

MEMORIAL DAY

Evening

and all the graves

are full

The flags

have stone stars

and stone stripes

Today the sun above

Lake Erie was alive

We danced over rocks

and lay warm in the sand

The moon

and Evening News

will not

come out tonight

in memory of us

SON

follow the many winding
inner streams
half sleepless nights
approach the far side
of each lake
half in deep shadow
reach the other side
before the sun
follow your father
thru the entrance
growing older calmer
every night
at last the same age
half in dream
go thru this entrance
to the holy room
follow him
drawn here by
time before
time after
follow and enter

STOP STABBING CRABGRASS

Stop stabbing crabgrass
with your killer cane
go in   though TV's dull
your thrill was Ruby
shooting Oswald live
Pick up your phone
and dial death's
recorded message
out your picture window
watch the flying vulture
eyeing the flamingo
on your lawn
in bed turn the electric
blanket up and up
asleep you'll never
hear us knock
and won't feel guilty
not to let us in
We're standing out here
cold as bayonets
rain running down our faces
Inside it must be dark
we cast long shadows
on your windows

DRAG TREES ALONG THE SNOW

Drag trees along the snow

and pile them high

(the bon fire maker's flames

spring at the sky

and light our circled faces

from the outer dark

fire spreads through our mountain

trees explode with cracks

backs cold the fire thrusts

our arms warm around each other

trees burn down to ash

descend upon us gently)

walk away in snow

knowing what has burned

believing what remains

HIS FEET ARE FLAT

His feet are flat

and vast

       he cries

a lot inside his eyes

and turns his clown

cart one more wheel

his nose lights up

at night as red

as blood

           our laughter

streaks his thick

white cheeks

LOW HOUSES WHITE ALONG THE STREET

low houses white along the street

dark shops all shut

the silent folk walk forth

and back in their grey footprints

die too soon too late

before their birds soar

after waking from their dreams

their lives are nothing else

paint the houses white each fall

lock the shops at dusk

walk the streets

toeprints heelprints the same

remember dreams

listen for wings

THEY'LL NEVER FIND

They'll never find

a grave to hold him

or a stone to hold

his name

        Pablo

Diego Jose

Francisco de

Paula Juan

Nepumoceno

Maria de los

Remedios

Cipriano de la

Santisima

Trinidad

Ruiz y

        Picasso

HELL IS MEASURED IN MEN

hell is measured in men
heaven in minutes
what time are I and you
I forget people and
expect them to remember me
I take for granted warmth
beneath the blanket til
the snow blows on my face
this was a good day one of those
hard to believe good days
you took me with your lips
sang through me with your fingers
we played the record where Bill
Evans says it all tells us how
sad our happy nights can be
hell is measured in remember
heaven in believe
safe from shelter
standing in our falling tears
making lonely circles
saying love   too many people
all the trees are gone
what time are I and you
tell me where the big hand
is   the little hand
and I'll show you what
earth we happen on

CALLEY

Calley over your breast pocket
mine said Keller   I was twenty
at Fort Benning   forty now
I never got to war but wore
the same bars on my shoulders
same crossed rifles I was
ready then to use   Korea or
wherever I was sent   I spent
the war in snowed-in Pennsylvania
Bill Calley we're all killing you
for what I would have done
I wouldn't do it now   I wouldn't
wear the bars or enter any war
that's easier at forty than at
twenty though   easier in nineteen
seven one than five one
I hear that sometimes you're a
normal guy   considerate   compassionate
we've had a taste of your obedience
'when all's in anger' someone told
Coriolanus 'you make strong party
or defend yourself by calmness
or by absence'   all's in anger and
we're all at fault   we kill someone
he must be enemy   if he's not enemy
then what's he doing dead
when you were at Fort Benning
Calley   did they still call it
the Benning School for Boys
did they still have those
bayonet drills flesh to steel
did they still teach you to
beware civilians bearing gifts
while you were there someone was
killing off civilians at an awesome
rate in Nam   now hurry up it's

time to patch ripped consciences
let's make the patches out of
Calley's faded stained fatigues
I don't believe in war Bill
but in one you can't act
as if you're out   you were so wrong
you reek   you're rotten
but the rest of us
smell just as bad   I'm glad
I've had these twenty years
to freely change my mind in
you ought to have them too

IN HIS WORLD PASSERS BY

in his world passers by

are targets   fear and

tears to laugh at   stones

to throw   nothing living

left he stones the dead

all midnight through their

fences   stone hurting stone

in his world street lights

smash and birds from high

nests shatter with the glass

nothing living left he breaks

wine bottles   punctures tires

and stones the dead all

midnight through their fences

stone hurting stone

SUE

in soft domed rooms

behind her sleep

boys wearing only

          laughter

shrug at her door

they enter fumbling for

          her name

they probe and gasp

her memories awake

they look down on her

          paleness

and they leave

haunted by the sadness

they put in her eyes

GEORGE

This feels like dream
or waking from long sleep
the morning
　　　George was seventeen
went on for sixty years
he walked unknown
tall among taller strangers
slept four hours to
breathe the thin sour air of dawn
hearing no words from no companion
watching himself sweat
reaching for sleep as for a woman
living without one and the other
in two months George
spoke a hundred words
　　　later talked less
not stupid never unaware
dressed and undressed in dark
needed no watch to tell him
it was late
no mirror to remind him
he was grey
lived in an unmarked grave
behind the kitchen of a　　　stone three storey tomb
　　　he never had to climb the stairs
　　　window propped open with a stick
　　　to let night drop its
　　　cold white ashes on his sill
　　　This feels like dream
　　　or waking from long sleep
　　　this morning
　　　　　snow turns over over in the sky
　　　and George is dead
　　　a little quieter than always
　　　casket much too fancy
　　　much too empty

stone stairs to be descended
cautiously with fragile aunts
a banner hung from each antenna
funeral
headlights turned on
snow falling filling streets
prayers muttered into scarves
    as George is lowered
into iron earth
a few of these
flakes flicker whitely
through his open window

THE THREE SHEEP HUDDLE

The three sheep huddle

against the fence one

behind another like a

train hugging a

mountainside

The eight brown ducks

stay close to shore

and to each other But

the goat

placid on his sun-

baked rock gives me

some hope today will

not be frightening

OCTOBER DAY

1

Peanut butter
jelly cracked
wheat bread
and cokes
inside the car
then Jim and
Bob and I
hop over wind
splashed rocks
excited letting
this wild lake
throsh up on low-
down logs
and even splush
our boot toes
as our once quiet
Octopus' Garden's
overwashed with
leaps of spray

2

Quiet after warmth and dinner
and the boys gone home
that night I trailed the sunset
from marina to marina
all along Niagara Street
beneath great purple birds of cloud
parking to watch the downing light
between pale interludes of rain

NOVEMBER NIGHT: TREES

I laughed so many poems
talked of trees
      against the sky
but look – the way that
long lombardy's etched
the way the bare few elms
      dance tableau black on grey
a lean of birch
      a spread and stretch of maple
leaves clinging longer
than any in my memory
streets lights like
nippled gumdrops
lumine lacy greywork
      needled witchery
strong hurl of heavy
      barkdark limbs
a flowing stillness in each reaching
silhouette   well
here's another poem
from a former scoffer
trees against the sky

THREAD

"He who holds me by
a thread is not strong;
the thread is strong."
                    - Antonio Porchia

It's not a chain
I know chains well
I hold my hands this way
because of chains
I rub my wrists sometimes
and feel the steel clasp
of the chains' strange
absence

I'm still bound to you
by a thread
thin fine but strong
it cut my fingers
when I tried to break it
bled in thin fine lines
like memories I tried
not to remember

In our new darkness
blindness is a strength
and hands are eyes
my wounded fingers
walk to you along the thread
to try again its fine
strong cruel beauty

YOU CAN

I'm sorry, Thomas
Wolfe. I know you can
go home again.
And like the other
things I know,
I'll never prove it.
But you can. There
is no point
of no return. There
is a point
which, passed,
means you can
live in past
or any time.
Tonight I reached
that point.
I went back, I
stood, one foot inside
the warm familiar hall.
I knew, as sure
as snow was falling
in the dark, I
could have stayed.
There was a mindless
thing inside my heart
that knew, that
felt it, in
the shuffled eyes
of those beloved strangers,
in their gentle,
awkward,
hesitant reclosing
of that finite door.

FAUN

A flute song rises
from where you lie
        along warm rock
(where human ends
        where animal begins)
rises in warm lazy curves
from where you lie
        among white roses
dreaming that you dream
longing as hot heavy noon
envelops you in light
        (half-voicing your
half-animal desire)
lids shut
        prolonging your sweet vision
like a warm statue
awakening to flesh and trees
to disappearing goddesses
        caressed in memory
shimmering beyond your opened eyes
One's eyes were blue
        cold as springwater tingling
one murmured like a breeze
        along your thigh
both disappeared before they
could be flesh touched by
your fingertips and lips
Haunted by muted half-heard music
through the dream white glade
bending glide aimlessly
        through branches leaves
but never leave your dream
embrace it kiss it shamelessly
caress those soft-edged memories
let music flow
        from lips to breasts to lips

(warm lazy animal)
your flute song rises from
the soft ledge where you dream

DRIVING THROUGH THE
FINGER LAKES REGION

Ages back the glacier's skinny fingers
printed lakes into this land
and still the winter waters unchill slowly
though the April sun springs
across ageless hills now grey brown
silver green grey silver brown
and aging men turning pale faces from their
crumbling shanties sit and watch
the hopeless river move unhurrying
toward nowhere toward Owego
where the only life is that imprinted
by Indians before they left their village
of Owagea an age ago   The homeless hills
descend on villages and climb away
moving on roads our car decides to take
obedient to signs we watch for deer
along the Thruway but see only an endless
river of cars   Oh we go nowhere sixty
miles per hour   obedient to radios
we set our watches forward saving daylight
from extinction   our car aims us arrow-like
at Buffalo

AFFECT

And so I reawaken
        in your dawn
groping   trying to grow
feeling the morning
        slither through your fields
reaching like branches
        or like roots
to know what you
perhaps have always touched

Your web of questionings
        is delicately intricate
it weaves itself of fine
        transparent hairs
I hush to hear the wonder
of your fields at noon
        I brush aside tall waftures
to seek your answers
        here behind the naked grass

Sitting above your evening
like a great sad owl
        watching my doorway
fill with falling leaves
        I try to finally absorb
the darkening magic of your sky
to feel the texture of
        forever with your hands

YOU SIT PETITE IN ALL

You sit petite in all

      my hallways

asking shyly why I'm sad

Womanchild you haunt

      me pleasantly

you're like a cool soft

scissors cutting through

Your voice and you

      can sink like

feathers float like stones

With nervous grace

your song climbs every stair

from your freeprison well

to my barred balcony

KAWABATA

"A silent death is
an endless word"

He lived so many evenings
(in his house of flesh)
on the secluded beach
            of little wind
watching the inevitable sea
prepare its final tide

While his orphaned childhood
limping on small
            bleeding feet
across snow countries
            in his mind
left unmistakable and
solitary tracks
for him to walk in
stalking his small
            wounded shadow
through his inmost
            patriarchal fields

Till a new snow quickly filled
the small red footprints
in the fields (and filled
the rooms he lived in)
And the long anticipated
            seaswell
overwashed the empty beach
            like any other tide

IDA LUPINO

In this film

she plays both Hamlet

and her mother's Ghost.

The shadows know

she is not walking

nervously tonight.

The closeups make

pure use of

her pure silence.

Her strength

gets in the way

of parody.

She is an empty-olived

icy very dry

martini tangueray.

CAN I SAY THIS IN WORDS

can I say this in words
say that your silence
converses with my
silence as we read
say that my
                typewriter is
compatible with
your TV / say that
your hand whispers
into my hand as
a movie
            moves us
both in different ways
say that in bed
we know bodies
together better
                than we know
body alone
say that share is
not what you
or I have coming
say that share is
what we do with
and without words

THE POEM ABOUT HUMPHREY AND THE LEAVES

It's so quiet sitting looking at the fallen
leaves outside the study window it will only
be October for a few days yet Monday will be
Halloween and this is Wednesday in the leaves
I'm well not quite as tired as I might be my
papers all are finished I brought no work
home for a change it will be dark in two hours
where the leaves are but I'll have one slow
drink and eat some rice before it gets
completely dark the rice is cooking slowly and
there's water running from the bathtub faucet
not just dripping children running through the
leaves last night on TV Humphrey went back to
the Senate looking old and sick and senators
embraced him kissed him right there in the
Senate just imagine all these leaves have
fallen speeches praised him praised he got up
said and said it smiling two kids just came
to my side door collecting for United Way the
evening paperboy has not arrived yet plowing
through the leaves but I began to say that
Humphrey listened to the praise and then said
Oh I'm old enough to know that all these things
you've just said aren't true but I'm just
weak enough that right now I believe them all

FOR A VERY YOUNG
BLACK GIRL WHO DIED

I don't know much
about you / I mean
I don't know your
name or even what
city you lived in
my friend told me
you were only
seven?
and you had Sickle
Cell Anemia
he said that you
were on the Bus
arriving at your
newNEW schoolSCHOOL
(I'll bet you were
scared / at seven
I'd have wet my
pants)
the doctor later
said - my friend
told me – that any
one with Sickle Cell
reacts! extremely! to
emotional! stress!
I guess your death
was "understandable":
you and a few poor
little other kids
(all "happened"
to be black)
tensing inside that
yellow Bus: keeping
each other from crying
– that might only make
it worse – and

outside SCREAMING
Half a Thousand
Whitefolks (I'm white
with shame) CHANTING
:Go Back Where You Came
From / GO BACK WHERE
YOU CAME FROM / **GO
BACK WHERE YOU**

DIS IN TE GRA TION

Dis in te gra tion
a mild formal word for
fall ing a part come
ing a part not neatly
not at the seams but
every where at once a
molecular dys en ter y

Dis integrity? Does integrity
dis in te grate in that
debilitating diarrhetic way?

Dis in ter est ed is a
calm and passive word
but dis in ter
exhumes us from passivity
digs up the still intact
integrity that was in ter
red with our bones

ALWAYS A LEGACY

in memory of my Father

ye are the	Loss is hard
	but stirs a thing
salt of the	in us which
	strengthens
earth: but if	makes us
	grow inward
the salt have	a parent leaves a
	double legacy
lost his savour	in living in
	dying
wherewith	That's as it
	should be
shall it	as the generations
	go
be salted	always a legacy
	to the living

A DARK TIME

A dark time
darker because my
eyes are open
in this room
where they seldom were
only just after and
just before sleep
and bleary then
or when we made love
in the dim light the
sudden closenesses
tall nipple deep navel soft
curling hairs surrounded
my open eyes
I always went to sleep almost
as I pressed the pillow
but tonight I'm stubborn
it's almost painful
keeping my eyes open
so I do
looking at nothing
dark air vague ceiling
for you to materialize
like this dark time
growing out from your
absence: a coarse black
whisker from a mole

I SEE ME WASHING MY GREY

I see me washing my grey
emptiness with bourbon-on
the-rocks from an ornate
decanter while Chet
Baker's horn cries
"Wish You Love" the
maudlin mourning after
you leave
I'd rather carry you
carefully in a
simple container
out on the rocks of
Joe's Head under
circling grey seagulls
at sunset
and scatter you
let ocean breezes
blend you with
waves' rhythms
permanence of rocks
gulls' cries

TINY DOTS OF SNOW DRIFT

Tiny
     dots of snow   drift
separately
past these three windows
like the silences
that Morton Feldman wrote
for Frank O'Hara
      Just as spring
began to be
       mildly possible
these white ellipses appear
to prove its absence
     and foreshadow yours
as if I needed
punctuation
marking off the empty
     and the nearly empty
spaces in my
winter's tale

SALUTATORY 1969

We walked through halls untouching

wrapped tightly in each other's presence

breathing for your mother whose breath stopped

the night before I don't remember now

if you were in your gown and cap

or in the pretty dress you wore beneath it

seems important to remember and I can't

We didn't care for once about the eyes

we were so right they didn't matter maybe they

had never mattered to you You were so beautiful

giving your salutatory speech my breath

still catches eight years later watching you

MY CIRCLES

1   Drop
    a stone
    (any shape)
    in a pond
    (any shape)

2   my mother's old
    silly song: spring
    would be a dreary
    season were there
    nothing else but
    spring would be a
    dreary season were
    there nothing else
    but

3   Hepworth moving for
    two decades in a
    straight line turns
    the white marble music
    of her Sphere Atop Two
    Segments to the holy
    silence of the open-
    ings (see sky through)
    in her Porthmeor: Sea
    Form

4   Lonely hold
    lonely stroke
    down lonely
    up lonely
    lonely stroke
    lonely flow

5   Dial seven numbers
    let the phone ring
    seven times dial
    seven numbers let the
    phone ring seven times
    dial

6   Bowl cupped
    in warm hands
    holds tea leaves
    steeping
    in hot water

NOTES TOWARD NEW COMMANDMENTS

Listen love
Thou shalt not be so honest
with those who prize hypocrisy
Thou shalt not be so loving
with those who are scared they
might like you if they tried
Thou shalt not be so kind
so generous with those too proud
and too embarrassed to receive
Thou shalt

Oh love you must know what I mean
Thou shalt not be thyself
because people are talking about you
all those people who think they
know you so damned well and
well
they resemble the orifice
in their own derriere
but hell I guess we all do sometimes

Listen love
if you still want to
try to reach them
dial two
seven seven
four six five three
be ready to hang up in case
the obscenities start but
if a human voice answers
take a chance –
it might be me

SO WE CLIMB HIGHER

So we climb higher
than people can
and lie together
breathing heaven
on the mountain top
So we touch deeper
than people can
and reach the very
center of the earth's
warm joy So we hold
a miracle between
our thighs and in
our arms So when
we wake there's
my hand sweating
into your hand and
your head pressing on
my sunburnt shoulder:
So we're human
after all

I WANT TO TALK ABOUT YOU

A field of golden

grass fills with tall

pink-petaled flowers

I return to meditations

I have never left

Lights ripple through me

silently across calm water

I whisper to an empty

pillow in the dark

I WANTED TO GIVE YOU

I wanted to give you
green fields full of
purple loosestrife
black skies filled
with stars
A moment after waking
I can almost separate
the dream parts
from the real
Thicker than tears
sadder than water
your blood flowed out
on your pillow
dark red
on that white cloth
I thought Porchia's words:
"When your suffering is
a little greater
than my suffering
I feel that I am
a little cruel"
What could I give you?
empathy? bandages?
We staunched the blood
You smiled
around your pain
and reassured me
When I insisted
I had given nothing
you wrote me an IOU
for loosestrife
an IOU for stars
Here they are See?
written on my pillow
written in dark red
on this white cloth

RIDING THROUGH THE NIGHT

Riding through the night
together from somewhere,
unimportant where, the
dark road, familiar to
our headlights, winds back
toward the ocean, and the
rocks, and toward our tent,
some ways more home than any
we have found. Or does it?
It's a haunting ride some
nights, less déjà vu than
glimpses of a journey we
may never cease to take.
Before long, the world will
take away most of the things
we love, even you away from
me. But some things last in
this life, and beyond, and
they must have to do with being
in this car with you on quiet
nights like this, riding toward
somewhere, doesn't matter where,
just riding through the night
together toward.

HALLOWE'EN EVE IN COURT

A Rumpelsnitz
for Sherry

Psyched up so often for post-
ponement   Almost unwilling to
believe the trial will be held
Cynical of master plans in
which we're ready till it counts
Wary of Tom Satan masquerading
as a "counsel" for "defense"
ready to catch us "people" with
our costumes off "defenses" down
and rip off more than masks
We're careful crossing parking
lots   We've been assaulted and
intimidated more than once
But we'll bewitch Tom Goblin
this time   Wait till he sees us
all coming at him confidently
riding our warm brooms

PHOTOGRAPHS

Early November
no snow yet
This bare grey
tree with branches
spoked into the
sky reflects in
this pale cold
blue creek becomes
a water wheel
We stand we sit
amid dry leaves
dry grasses your
light hair accepts
their colors and
the paler yellow of
a weeping willow
on the creek bank
Everything is clean
and clear this brown
blue morning crisp
as notes played on
an English horn
Add November to our
list of unexpected
gifts this year

THE S.P.C.S.E.O.C.L. BLUES
for Robyn

Through vertical grey lines
of rain through dusty multiple
horizons of venetian blindness
I see the house across the
parking lot is painted dark
green this fall after at least
four years of piss yellow
Between calls I'm humming
"Everybody's gone away"
but it's only your name
that's crossed out on all
the staff lists and your
mailbox with another name
taped to it and you who
"resigned as coordinator"
says the cheery bubbly news-
letter "to pursue new profes-
sional endeavors" O shit Robyn
I've been here too long
Everybody went away and
one of them by one I missed
but not like you
I should hum "Send in
the clowns" we really just
became friends when you were
already all ready to leave
I think "Send in the clowns"
I hum "Everybody's gone away...
Some gotta win some gotta lose
Goodtime Charley's got the blues"
Some gotta win some gotta lose
Goodtime Charley's got the
      Suicide Prevention and Crisis
      Services Emergency Outreach
      and Community Linkage
Blues

NOVEMBER HAS ONE POEM LEFT

November has three hours

left on my clock

The drapes are closed

to what the night

sky might announce

The telephone is

swollen silently with

reasons we won't call

An alto flute plays

clear dark phrases

rainbow sounds I

want you here to hear

My hands remember

leaving my gloves

in the car

November has one

poem left for you

EN OTRA CALLE

Mis pasos en esta calle
> At intervals of months
>> or years this dream

Resuenan
> of walking eyes closed through
>> the tunnel under the city

En otra calle
> not needing to see while
>> outside rain is falling

Donde
> walking comfortably
>> protected from the rain

Oigo mis pasos
> and always knowing my location
>> by the way my footsteps sound

Pasar en esta calle
> taut reverberations single sharp
>> soft notes in a nocturne climb descend

Donde
> a pleasant dream until tonight
>> my steps are silent and I feel

Solo es real la niebla
> cold drops of rain run down my neck

DEER PATH

We have waited in the north
as dawn crept toward us
Among these silver shadows
and listened to thin warmth
inhabit distant fields
small alone and cautious
have turned our furred hoods
close and muddled smoke grey breaths
the deer
Snow clouds
enshroud our deerhide footpaths
ears tuned to tiny silences
Reminiscence softens
deerslug rifles in our hands
quick between snowflakes and trees
What secret moving silhouettes
we seek in waking dreams
through the darkened stillness
What frigid polar vigils
we permit ourselves to keep
bounds past us quick silver

TRUE VALENTINES:
IN MEMORY OF
LOUIS ZUKOFSKY

Names are not always known,

nor soul's, intellect's,

vast troubled depth. Few

knew you, and those knew

most mind. Fewer knew heart,

and read the true Valentines

sent her, your Celia, sent

Paul, your son. Love lasts,

their message, by a small

sober reveler, read. Love

lasts, foregoes publicity,

walks on tip toes near media,

was solaced by music, worked

and suffered long, and love

was kind.

THE HOUSE BURNED

The house burned
down last night
after you left
through the south door
and I turned back
unwilling to face
your back becoming
darker and more distant.
The flames were green
and billowed grass-green
smoke and I retreated
north onto the neighbors'
crackling orange lawn
where someone wrapped me
whole, surviving, in a
coarse grey blanket
mourning, meditating,
shivering. I woke this
morning in the same
bed where the house
burned and you
departed southward
in the night. I have
so much to do now:
pay the neighbors for
lawn damage, buy someone
a new grey blanket,
account for all survivors,
wait for your return

THE WORLD IS BUILT OF

The world is built of

rotted garbage; the

world sucks. I know:

I read graffiti. But

this morning near the

parking lot I saw these

phlox, the first undan-

delion wildflowers I

have seen this spring.

They must have had to

fight their pinkish-

purple way up through

the weeds the paper bags

the broken glass. Well

what a lift they gave me

just before I had to drive

my battered rusty "Skylark"

back into graffiti land.

SUPPOSE THAT WE WERE

Suppose that we were

named as Cuckoo is, or

WhipPoorWill, by what we

say, or what we sing:

Would my name be

     AreYouAllRight?

Would yours be

     HowExciting!?

FOR DANA, IN WICHITA

Struggle through your
ragged middle-of-the-
night; the birds will
beat their mourning
wings against the pane:
'Dana, nous t'aimons.'
Cry, be bitter; little
kids will line side-
walks like birds: 'Dana,
nous t'aimons.' Flee the
scream that tears your
throat, scramble up the
stairs so damned, so
scared; the birds will
line up on the roof:
'Dana, nous t'aimons.'
Ride your lonely weary
nightmare: wake to
children's birdsong:
'Dana, nous t'aimons.'

THIS KID

this kid
used to make
these paper doves
that really looked
like doves flying
when he tossed them
out the classroom windows
my "responsibility"
as teacher
was to stop him
from flying them
even stop him
from making them
I really
loved them
I thought his
paper doves
were beautiful
the best things
created in that room
and / or
sent out of it
in many years

DAISIES

1

The
white
petals,
the
golden
eye,
of
the
day

2

Day's Eye
The flower
in some species
opens   reveals
a golden disc
at morning   re-
closes at
           evening.

3

Not tearing
petals off
I'd not do
that   But
single-petal-
pointing with
this fingertip
an old-new
pattern: Touch
she loves me
Touch she loves
me more   Touch
she loves me
Touch she loves
me more

Wildflowers

TRANE AND NAIMA

The music he played for her
made hairs rise on her neck
who had to separate the music
from the man to live with him
who taped the music studied it
discussed until asleep she'd be
awakened asked what instrument
it was he heard deep in
his own recorded solo
Naima soaring pure in memory
who knew he loved his music
more than her who helped him
kick drugs to get back to
music not to her
Naima soaring pure in memory
he called her Neet (short for
Juanita) more than Naima
who was his comfortable
earthy (glowing subtle handsome)
basic backyard folks
he told her matter of factly
while they shared a hoagie
he would marry her
and eight years later when he left
said only "Naima I'm going to
make a change" who felt it
coming felt him drift even
while near him even while beside
    disconnecting   not communi-
    cating   whose marriage mis-
carried like her pregnancies
he said he had things to do
he took his clothes and horn
years later he recorded with his
second wife the song named for
his first his favorite

          composition all his life
Naima soaring pure
          beyond memory
part of what he had become the
greater entity he was because
                              of her
          no more his wife
her tribute draped his coffined
body the dashiki brown and
white she sewed the night before
brown for the earth he came from
                    would return to
white for his music's purity
seeing his body draped in it made
hairs rise on her neck

TO BE

                    although in giving I must

to be or…

                    find that I have nothing

two unending threads

                    although in giving of myself

which intertwine

                    I find that I am nothing

weave ghostly webs

                    although despair is

around each other

                    poetry sometimes

twist untwist the strands

                    tomorrow comes after today

by which life clings

                    dawn follows midnight

to this pale certainty:

                    and finding I am nothing

I desire to become

TASTE: O'HARA'S NAKIAN

I hate this age. Great persons

do not knock at doors to come

see what we're doing. Here is

cold. So train yourself, ignore

it. An artist is alone but also

is with people, civilized. Art is

taste and aristocracy. Van Gogh

was an aristocrat of mind, of

taste, that's what makes Picasso great.

Anyone can draw, model. To have

taste is to know exactly where

to place line, color.

VINCENT AND FRANK

Beautiful

　　　dancers grow

gracefully old,

dead poets find

　　　　words

by which to

　　　live.

Hermit Island

1

The bird the first morning
(a greyfoggy one) a tiny
thing that tiptoed the long
length of Head Beach
ahead of my damp sandaled plod
retreated in tiptoe panic
as a wave swashed up the beach
then made a timid sortie
onto shiny sand where waves
receded   to pick up tidbits
ocean left   At my end
of the beach the tiny
tiptoe creature turned
remembered it had wings I guess
and gracefully flew out above
the empty beach   I stood
sandbound and watched it
out of sight

2

Mrs. Clancy's
home-baked muffins
at the Kelp Shed
a morning ritual
some people
scoff and say 'that isn't
camping' but it feels right
sitting eating muffins
drinking tea
and looking out on Head
Beach in the sun or
rain the cold or
warm planning
the day: a walk out
on the rocks? a quick
cold swim? a shopping
trip to L.L. Bean? a
drive to Falmouth? or
Arrowsic? or Boothbay?
a book excursion to Cooks
Corner? then cook our
dinner on a wood fire
but one more muffin
first please Mrs. C.

Silence

is the sound

between the waves

Hear it?

And hear the

waves breaking

the silence?

Night is a time

for listening

to silence

and to rhythm

time for feeling

waves and being

sand washed

rhythmically by

waves and

breathing every

pungent silence

just before the

waves plunge

into it

      over it

breaking it

4

Say it: you can't really get
tired of – even see enough of –
rocks and green growing things
and the blue and white of ocean
and the very different blue
and white of sky. And here
the rocks are many-layered
vertically, and full of
magnificent colors: stripes and
striations of silver and coral
and pale grey and beige, dark
red and gold and bronze, pink
and dark grey and stark white.
And wildflowers surround our
campsite: I don't know the names,
but delicate pale yellow petals
and vivid purple cylinders, and
spiky balls of lavender, and
gleaming spots of gold, low
white circles and gold petals
around a clear brown center.

GREY MORNING
AFTER ALL NIGHT RAIN

every

thing is low

within reach

sky leans on rocks

presses

sand flat and hard

tiny sandpipers

kitter along the beach

among damp little heaps

of kelp

smell lingers   clings

pressed low by greyness

gulls forgetting wings

walk

walk with stiff dignity

then heavy

slow to rise

barely skim the level beach

only waves windblown high

and white

roll   and smash

and foam

6

Graffiti in the
    toilet house:
JM + HR – 6/24/75
      -- 11:00 AM –
That's the way kids –
pinpoint the moment   There
aren't too many and they
      don't last long

7

I have called it a grain
in the rocks
like the grain in wood
but it is a flow
caused by the flow
of water over many
years I guess
I like to walk along it
and feel that I
am moving with that flow
The rocks are sometimes
just outcroppings
domes of rock above
the little hilltop meadows
sometimes huge
extending many feet
becoming a whole
long island
all one great flow
or grain from one
end of the rock
to the other end
The colors are
so varied
These I'm sitting
in the grass next to
are chalky grey
and streaked
and grained with
coral
     silver
          darker grey
pale green
        and rusty iron
and as I start to walk
along the hilltop

rock ends
descends into sand
and then a few feet
farther on
emerges with that
same grain flowing
as if right through earth
right underground
and then
                visibly
on the hilltop surface
again   It flows
uphill –
or am I walking
"against the current" –
no the flow
goes down the other
side
then up and over
other rock outcroppings
What a lovely flow it is
everything bushes fissures
paths move with the flow
that wind and water
must have made
The tide is out
of the groove worn
into the center of this
group of rocks
making visible
the grain worn
in the rocks that
will be covered
at high tide the
flow of the whole
groove up into the land
I walk across the
grain / breaking the /
flow / conscious / of it /

feeling it as more than
vaguely unpleasant un-
natural but wanting
to get to the other
hilltop meadow my
favorite place to walk
I'm walking parallel
with where I walked before
but back the way I came
-- against the flow? –
no the flow is in the
rock
etched deeply
deeply in the rock
it flows as well this way
as back the other –
for the eye at least
But when my feet
arrive out on the
furthest jut
and I'm joined here
by five gulls
so white they make
the ocean even bluer
rocks even darker
and I turn around
I find that I was wrong
the flow moves only back
the other way
It is the tides
have carved this
grain so deep
incredibly deep in
these rocks
and the strength
is in the water
plunging at the shore
washing up and over it
not in the receding

fading ebb
The colors here are of
the ocean
less bleached out
than on the other hill
Dark water colors
kelp shades seaweed
tones   black
                    dark grey
deep green   deep brown
and always everywhere
these tiny flecks of
silver
so I walk *with* the flow
again knowing for sure
I'm not against
the current now
and watch the rocks
begin to bleach again
and then descend
and disappear in sand
and I sit down on a
warm sunwarm
silver stone
carefully to avoid
poison ivy
and feel a little
little bit
a part of all
this majesty
and strength and
grace   I know at least
how natural and good
it is to join the flow

8

Warm

watching scraps of wood

(from Washburn's lumber yard)

burn quickly in our

flashle cracking fire –

smoke blackening

the massive rock

behind the lashing flames –

we sat there near our tent

out on Joe's Head

and didn't see

the night lights of the

Prince of Fundy

move slowly past

heading for Nova Scotia

through the dark Atlantic

cold

9

I woke up in the middle of the night
with an urgent need to piss – barely
threw on some sandals and pants in my
hurry, and didn't put on my glasses.
Stumbling up the path to the john, I
noticed nothing unusual, but after the
relief of my physical discomfort, what
a revelation to emerge into the incred-
ible darkness with the highest, vastest
sky full of stars I had ever seen! Even
without my glasses, they were startlingly
clear and recognizable. How I could ever
have had trouble identifying constellations
before was hard to imagine. The sense of
nearness and of immeasurably great distance
were both brilliantly evident – what a
feeling! I was dizzy with pride of ownership
and with humility and insignificance, simul-
taneously.

10

One more full day here
Pack up tomorrow morning
And then another year
maybe more than one this time
But the place gets to be part
of the person
                You take it
with you in some ways
the sounds
                and silence
especially
                the feeling
of permanence
                    the stillness
and the rhythms / the movement
The waves stay with you
Waves
ever-changing things
no two alike
suddenly crashing
washing and foaming
up the beach
                suddenly gone
But never gone
In change is permanence
                    The sound
stays / the beauty stays
the tidal rhythm stays
Stays here at Hermit Island
stays on every ocean coast
and stays with me
away from here / from ocean
for a year
                or longer
if I need

A RICHER ALLEGIANCE

I find the story* I've been
looking for and copy the last
paragraph to show to you:

> I wondered how many women, fresh
> from the excitement of a lover...

>> every spring white roses appear
>> that my father planted many years
>> ago this rain today looks like
>> tears on these white petals white
>> roses don't have eyes or mouths
>> but still they see and taste the
>> clean soft wonder of the rain

"I cried a tear' Anne Murray's voice
sings on the stereo 'you wiped it dry
I was confused you cleared my mind'

>> The phone rings and unbelievably
>> it's the person who was the catalyst
>> for everything that's mattered in
>> our life these last incredible
>> eleven days he talks I talk about
>> some trivial things that would
>> have been significant before

> I wondered how many women, fresh
> from the excitement of a lover,
> or from the frustration of
> timidity, and keen with hope for
> the future, or blind with despair
> at the present, succumb to the acceptable
> and inexacting arms of their husbands?
> - and have they not felt, in moments
> of wild inconsolation, traitors to
> a richer allegiance?

we've made love like these
white roses and this rain we've been
as clean as gentle as they are
we've felt as pure we've touched
each other's petals with our
secret rain and washed each other
with our tongues   hands   tears
and springing laughter

'and held me up' Anne sings
'and gave me dignity you
needed me you needed me'

I think of reading him the passage
I just copied see if the catalyst
can recognize the process he began
the miracle I don't I say yes to an
invitation to his house this Friday
clean my glasses carefully hang up the
phone I picture you in inexacting arms
I play Anne's song and watch white
roses cry

* "The Party,"
by Dachine Rainer

274

LOVERS

The bumper stickers
about great lovers
are all wrong.
English teachers are
the greatest lovers.
Who else would
make you do it
over and over
again and again
until you get it right?
Who else would
lean on one elbow,
look you over thoroughly
and whisper: "In, out, under, over,
Oh, I love your prepositions!"

"What sends a lonely
frightened child into
its mother's arms is
need and what is given
back is love." Well yes
but that's too narrow,
that excludes. Love sends
that child to hug its
mother (not just loneliness
and fright) and what the
mother gives is given
out of need as well as
love. "The opposite of
love is not hate, it is
fear." I don't know much
of hate. I try hard not
to feel it even in
others. But I've been
intimate with fear and
it's more like accompaniment
than like an opposite of
love. Fear is an
unfamiliar mattress for
love's bed, a troubling
breeze through love's
half-open window,
but it's there. Try
loving me or letting me
love you without some
fear. Try loving God.

I struggle with my lows
You help me learn a new role
comic this time
while we both play other roles:
who people think we are
who we should want to be
who conscience lets us be
who we think we'll be happy being
This "architect"'s not hard to play
the words and stage directions
                    are explicit
a pompous oaf like other "architects"
                    who have no subtlety
                    deserve no sympathy
I struggle with my lows
This one's discouragement with memory
let's keep it on that surface
It wasn't there while we read
                    Act One earlier
but it's here after talk
                    of sorrow   loss
                    and poetry
Face them and I can't concentrate
                    on memorizing farce
Good explanations   want some more?
I manufacture explanations
they make sense
they nearly satisfy you
you pretend they do
                    smile gently   leave
I struggle with my lows

NOSTALGIC INNOVATIONS

Sometimes when we
don't touch
for a day
or two
it's seldom longer
my body
half remembers
half imagines
joining yours
in old-new combinations
nostalgic innovations
and when we
really touch again
it's like we're
playing music
we have heard before
but neither we nor
anyone has ever
heard it played
like this

DAY AND NIGHT

Your note says you
woke in the night
relaxed and peaceful
remembering our
loving in and
out of dreams
then slept again
to wake this morning
to more dreams
sending the same
silent (invisible?) calm
all through you
as if day and
night were not
different at all

POEM FOR ROBYN

Hands talking touching
driving back we realize
this Stratford day has
made this difference:
at its end we're
really friends
can talk about the man
you left in San Diego
and don't want to see
when you vacation there
the woman I make total
love with but
can't marry
even share in words
the touching splendor
of past present loves
This morning we shared
bridge tolls peaches talk
from Buffalo to Stratford
by way of San Diego
this festive afternoon saw
acrobatic wrestlers share the stage
with gross and tender lovers
good bad poems picked
by loving fingers
from trees free
in a magic forest
Driving back
here in this moving
August darkness
fingers talk to friendly
fingers about hands
that are not here

IS IT

After midnight

songs seem to come

from a closet

I walk quickly past

afraid to intrude

stop at a

respectful distance

listen

songs are muffled

but I think I hear:

Why is there

no color in coming

in silence

in a lonely cry

no color in going

in ghosts

I need someone's ear

when I talk

someone's mouth

when I listen to

who is it you

is it you

BREL DIED THURSDAY

"Perhaps you feel too
much and maybe that's
a crime   Perhaps you
pray too much and there
isn't any shrine"
                    - Jacques Brel

Brel died Thursday
and I never spoke
to him and wouldn't
have if he had lived
But he was more like me
than my brothers or
my closest friends
His vision wasn't me
but his intensity
Brel died Thursday
but it's you I have
to speak to love
because half those
words that Brel and I
have never said
I'll whisper
now he's dead
Brel died Thursday
Like Coltrane after
his death some
will pray to Brel
Like Trane I won't
be one   And not because
there isn't any shrine
I'll go on praying where
I am: Thank you for
helping me talk back to
voices on the crisis phones
do more for those I love
and try to write

these new words
in the night
Brel died Thursday
we're alive and if
I feel too much
you smile and murmur
"scant the excess"
if I pray too much
I think you'll whisper "well
he was a friend of Brel"

ANSWERS

Time to think

sometimes means

time to worry

Right now I'm

asking myself

questions not

unimportant but

not urgent as

I'm making them

questions that

begin   When will

           Where do

           How can

I answer them

myself   Some day

           Some place

and   Oh so carefully

TRANE AS OMNEDARUTH

Brett – It's what people
have instead of God.
Jake – Some people have
God. Quite a lot.

What the King Bishop
Ha'qq's congregation
has instead of God is
Omnedaruth, the music and
the spirit of Coltrane.
Listen to *Dear Lord* or to
A Love Supreme – Trane's
ultimate love songs to
God – and almost feel what
Ha'qq's believers feel:
The music is Compassion
Omnedaruth the music is
the man transcends the man
becomes Compassion through
the music worship Omne-
daruth mindlessly adore
His holy name. A man like
Coltrane had God quite a
lot, transcended all of us,
you hear that, feel his
music pray. The man is
worshiped and prayed to
as Omnedaruth now
          A reluctant mystic,
he wanted only to be
John Coltrane.

WAY OFF BROADWAY #2

Sitting in the

dressing room

(school cafeteria)

made- up and costumed

for scene one

it's quite a shock

to find this lipstick

on my coffee cup

and realize that

it's my own

WELCOME

Under but so close to surfaces

we hear familiar melodies

becoming waves of light

and streams of energy

flowing strongly between layers

between lives between

this life and mystery

back to sources

toward whatever

ultimate beauty and beyond

discovering relationships

under but so

close to surfaces

changing their familiarity

expressing them in waves

of light and streams of

energy

YELLOW

This Friday afternoon I'm
looking at these yellow flowers
remembering you gave them to me
on a distant Saturday
They refuse to wither
act as if they'll last
a month of Mondays
on this table in this glass
Their leaves their green parts
withered and were thrown
away one brownish Thursday
but not the russet
and the yellow flowers
After one too many Wednesday
the russet ones dried down
and dropped into a
plastic kitchen bag
The yellow ones still
glow here in this glass
upon this table like our
faces glowing in a Sunday
mirror after love
Some distant Tuesday even
the yellow flowers will wither
but we'll remember them
and glow a little extra
each loveday for at least a week

WAY OFF BROADWAY #3

I'm out there under lights
the final scene
tuxed and homburged
playing a grumpy producer
apologizing awkwardly
to a triumphant actor I've tried
to remove from the play
and then I'm
in the dressing room
almost untuxed
accepting awkward plaudits
on my acting
from a director
who removed me
from the last play
I was in

OPEN LETTER TO BOBBY McGEE
TEN YEARS LATER

(with apologies to Kristofferson)

So Bobby you live halfway from
Salinas to that other town
and they are both a drag
and sure you love your kids
(and so would I) but Bobby your
old man's a digital computer up
in Monterey and calls you
"wifey" when he talks at all
and let's you wait on him
while he gets fatter and more
comfortable Well Bobby I know you
remember being with me on the road
faded out in Baton Rouge
miserable in New Orleans
and happy everywhere
just keeping both of us as warm
as possible and sharing anything
that we could scrounge
just singing up a storm of
happy blues songs every afternoon
maybe freedom felt like losing then
but no we could be free together

feeling good would

still be good enough and I don't

even have to ramble anymore

I'm ready to stay with you and

your kids wherever and

whenever you decide

and if you just can't do it

well I still want you to

know this Bobby love I let you

go the last time cause I thought

that it was best for you but no

What's best for us is us and

Bobby I would never

let you slip away again

BETWEEN

These lonely hours between

are strange

emptied of the sharing that has

filled our days for these two

dozen weeks

the magic thrill as tips of

bodies touched

the wondrous warmth as

fluids merged and blended

the stimulating soothing

unforgotten words

the budding limbs we

walked beneath

the golden petals

we luxuriated near

all emptied now

except in poignant memory

in these strange lonely

hours between

WEATHER

A voice on radio speaks of
betrayal by the weather and
it's raining very hard
against my windows lighted
by my faithful courtyard lights
as I look past poinsettia
sentries out to that too-warm
too-windy mid-December after-
midnight anything is probable
but here inside my citadel
the basement floor is dry
and these mums ought to
stand guard loyally in
spite of brownish under-
petals if my thermostat
has only been set right

NEW YEAR'S EVE

nineteen seventy

ni- eight until

midnight and the

crumbs in the

snow and the

seed in the cages

and the BALL

in TIMES SQUARE

and the beaks in the

branches and the slopped

drinks and the de-squawked

noisemakers and the

chirps in the air and the

more or less living

relatives of Guy

Lombardo are all

for the birds

"GUESS WHO"

I promised me I'd be
in bed by now
and here I am
typing words I haven't
written yet and
feeling things I
haven't thought
while another midnight
sneaks up on me from
behind, puts a woman's
hands across my eyes –
I think they're your
hands, love – and
whispers the predictable
predicted words

MOMENT

Were they still
singing in the
dark arena two
hours later the
many-colored dancers
who had finally begun
to move more mildly
through our synthe-
sizing minds after
hot tea and cool
cheese cake as we were
standing in my bare
hands near a corner
streetlight and we
kissed once
happy sad
with a little more
than lips I thought
for just a moment
that they still were
singing

THE LYRIC POET BREAKS
OPEN HIS FORTUNE COOKIES

You will outpour exuberant
emotion like Niagara Falls

You will usually perceive
and sometimes express with
beauty and lyricism

You will be subjective
and sensual and
lonely as hell

You will shed tears
intensely in your
egg drop soup

WORDS

There are words

that make it some

times

words that

would make it if

remembered when

needed

words that

are unnecessary but

which unexpressed

add depth to what's

expressed

words that

are familiar and are

mildly trite but

very reassuring very

warm

words that lose

meaning without warning

words that bandage

wounds that words have

made

words that sing

like music without

music

words that hurt

so terribly the speaker

wants to rip them back

from hearing ears receiving

minds

words that know their

own inadequacy

words that

suspect their own signifi-

cance

words that

words that words that

words

AFTER ACTING THE PRIEST
IN *THE RUNNER STUMBLES*

for Milan Stitt

saw the lilac

touched it always

touching. lilacs

grow when earth

is cold are here

when no one knows.

     Lilacs will be different this year will

     be survivors springing up from bloodwarm

     hearts through cold hard-crusted earth.

all those trees

and not a single…

birds leave – forest

fire. a long

time since a rainbow.

     Birds will be harbingers of green and

     plashy woodpaths under rainbows in

     a cool and sudden spring.

punish for compassion?
held you if you
cried. resist temptation
- to be human?
cruelty must stop.

      People will be younger older
      human now their tears accepted their
      ordinary kindnesses appreciated more.

finished book now
time to bring the
lilac promised.
like to read the
book. it's burned
destroyed.

      And this haunted sometime actor will
      return to writing poems that like
      lilacs have survived their drought.

TWO

Love words are
hard to write
must fit these
two strange
special people
trapped by love

This is so easy
why was I so
stupid

avoid that
pseudo-language
pseudo-lovers
loose upon each
other

I don't understand
why it seemed so
worthy

yet acknowledge
common love words
may be most true
most precise

I listen for your
steps in the
hall

WAITING

These hours I wait are
out-of-focus photographs
that don't appear in
albums, spill-stained
notes mailboxes never
get.
      Your Taurus horoscope
was much too accurate:
conflict at home.
             I meant
the empty words I said –
"I'm with you" – but still
you were there with conflict,
without me.
          These hours I
wait are tapes partly
erased by error, botched
rehearsals that postpone a
play.
      Your phone call was
uneasy: "I can't talk. It's
bad. I'm hanging in there."

These hours I wait I watch
them fall with rain: the
briefly deep pink blossoms
of the flowering tree.
            The
blossoms falling spatter
brick wall, clipped grass,
sidewalk. Scraggly clingers
stay. Fallen or hanging on,
they're limp and pale.

NOT QUITE MARRIED

There was our rising
tide, our overflow,
deep feelings of what
being married ought to be,
our sublime weariness, our
patient touching voyage
back into the tide, to
rise, to reach a greater
flowing-over. There were
kisses, whispers; peacefully
you slept. The clock said
three a.m. There were
children asleep to be
looked in on, lights up-
stairs and down to be
shut off, a backyard pool
to tend to, an outside
door to lock. There was a
silent moment looking at
the dark house full of
sleepers, my car to start, a
quiet drive back to my room.

FLUTE

"If you can

imagine some

thing you

can play it"

Let me be

    your flute

Rouse the

gods Soothe

all the

    nerve-ends

Expand our

      rainbow

Let it fill

      our sky

FLOWERS

1

Three flowers in a corner

of the field bordering the

parking lot: I noticed them

one workday morning in my

rear view mirror backing

out. They made

spring spring for me,

         belatedly,

beyond midMay. That night I

picked one, put it in water

here. I felt a little selfish.

But the field, world,

         still had two.

This flower's

    very much like you:

you love its color, pink

gently suffused with purple.

In this gold-leaf glass

    beneath the hanging lamp,

it seems to light the whole

apartment just as you do

    walking through the door.

People would call its beauty

delicate, and so it is: its

petals sensitive to finger tips

and eyes; the tiny center of each

blossom, cluster of pale green

    pale gold, formed –what's

the word? – exquisitely; again,

        like you.

3

The two phlox left in the

rained-on windblown field

are like you too. Strong,

durable, and tough. They

share your miracle: Since

when have strength and

durability, since when has

toughness been so lovely!

LISTEN

From the silver-grey sky

silver snowflakes fall

into no one's silence

into no one's poem

into these soft tangible

shadows lying in their

soft grey corners where

everything decides to

listen carefully to the

falling of each flake

WARM SLEEVE

We slip into the warm
sleeve of our love
Someone is crying
          in the night
nobody hears but us
We hold together what's
not known with what
          we feel
We touch, and turn the
stars on one by one

That night when all the
          stars go out
no one will know who
holds together what
and everyone will cry and
          no one hear us
slip into the warm
sleeve of our love

UNWILLING

My road away from you

winds through black trees,

each curve of road headlighted

as the car slows, feeling

its unwilling way away.

The only driver on this road

(like you, the only sleeper

in that bed), I feel I should

be driving in reverse, should

wind the road back on

its spool, returning and

returning me to you.

PRESENT TENSE

Some times just the
telephone itself is
too much I press it
too hard to my left
ear let my self get
too intense Five hours
at the Crisis
Service listening
to voices acu puncturing
my left ear drum "I
just flip out you
know it scares me I
don't even sometimes
know what's going down"
"My grandmother isn't
going to let me in My
mother threw me out I
have to go somewhere
you know" "It will be
terrible tomorrow They
call it a party I don't
know if I can face it"
"scares me" "have to go
somewhere" "it will be
terrible" I finally get
home and want to hide my
face between your
breasts and let you
soothe my left ear
wounds But all that we
have left today are
telephones I listen
and for a while it's
even good because it's
you and I do love you
present tense

WHAT YOU TEACH ME

Not hurry Not
feel we must
hurry Not lust
for Not grasp
at intense sens-
ations Not make
them goals

But to be patient. To be gentle.

Comfortable. To "take our time."

No matter what a clock thinks. To

accept our gradually growing

excitement. To let our spontaneity

mature: Be fully realized.

Not sudden e-
lation that
fades to de-
pression

But this fulfilled tranquility.

This flowering inside us: This

slowly bursting in upon us: Of our

love. And of this lasting peace.

SUNSHOWER

"The bright wet"
- Enslin

Washing off this

darkness with its

liquid light

Silencing this

silence

This morning's sun

is walking no it's

dancing through

this rain

DARK WATER

tired late Sunday nights
barely awake to drive
back to the Gap
getting near Harrisburg
(twenty-seven years before
Three-Mile Island) I'd
slowly grow aware of the
dark river: Susquehanna:
over there much too close
to the road in August I'd
begin to shiver cold and
think about the girl I'd
left 300 miles or anything
to stop that deep dark
river that still flows
beside me where I go

IMPATIENS

You showed me, yesterday,
tree-shaded flowers called
impatiens. They were lovely,
healthy, patient, as we were,
together, in that patient
little town.

Impatience n. The inability
to wait patiently. Restive
eagerness, desire, anticipation.

It was an afternoon for
savoring: we breathed in
bright red candles' straw-
berry scents; we laughed,
delighted with droll doll-
faces, card-faces; we
marveled at soil so rich its
stems support gigantic blooms.

Impatiens n. Any plant of
the genus Impatiens, which
includes the jewelweed. From
Latin "impatiens," IMPATIENT
(so called because the ripe
pods burst open when touched)

We smiled that we had only a

little money, even with the
Canadian exchange; I said I'd
tell every person in Niagara-
on-the-Lake how much I love you,
but I told only you, and only
thirty times; we savored moments
near hanging plants, near
petunia beds.

Jewelweed n. Any of several
plants of the genus Impatiens
having seed pods that burst
open at a touch when ripe.
Also called "touch-me-not."

We even "settled" semi-patiently
for goodbye kisses when our
little time ran out. Such patience.
That was yesterday. Today I'm
restive, eager; I anticipate; oh,
I desire! I feel an inability to
wait. Come savor me; I'll savor you.
I think we're ripe. Let's feel our
pods burst open when we touch.

CANTILENA

A thread of song

is being spun

in lovers busy

with their lovely

purposes, song

spun inside them

softly, in a soft

continuum, a

cantilena

without pause or

end, in language

without words,

spun as invitation

and as offering,

as deep eulogy,

as simple song.

SUMMER MORNING WALK

Starting out, still
dark, a glimpsed
white flower there,
a hint of yellow
here, a filmy silver
shawl over all of it,
more than sight a
feeling of brightening
sky, sunrise, fragrance
lifting with mist,
orange day lilies
cheer me from the road-
side, clear sunshine of
noon fulfills the
whispered promises
of dawn.

BIG DATE

Who can doubt

we are unique,

love? Our big

date Wednesday's

at the dentist's,

where you plan

to tell him that,

at our most loving

and climactic

moments, I

grind my teeth.

STRAWBERRY CANDLE

You've kept it secret under
garments in a drawer. But
one day its aroma's noticed,
and it's brought to light:
"What's this?" You choose
words carefully: "A candle,
strawberry-scented, from
Niagara-on-the-Lake. Doesn't it
smell nice?" The silence,
though expected, makes you
feel uneasy. What you haven't
said hangs in the air, a lie.
Through the guilt that muffles
scent and sound, you hear the
silence break: "Let's burn
that candle." "Oh, I like it
better as it is." "Let's burn
it. Isn't burning what a
candle's for?" "Well, some-
times a candle's not a candle.
Or more than a candle." "Huh?"
"I said, 'Sometimes –'" "Oh, I
heard what you said." The match
is struck, flame rises from the
wick. A smell of smoky wax
ascends and permeates. "I like
watching this candle burn."
You know that it will be watched
till it's dead. You're thankful
that it doesn't smell like
charred strawberries as it burns.

REQUIEM FOR A QUARTERBACK

Joe Gilliam
Didn't he play for the
     Steelers?
          a quarterback for the semi-pro
             Baltimore Eagles
Black quarterback? good
     passer?
        was found beaten on the head
          Monday night
Where should I put these
    white chrysanthemums?
       on the city's west side but the
            injury
On this table by the
      window?
      won't hurt his football abilities.
Here on the bookcase?
      He was lying on the street,
        bleeding from head wounds,
Do the roses look best
  on the coffee table?
      two men smashed his car windows
        with two-by-fours,
I like the way white flowers
   look in lamplight.
     but the injury won't hurt his
      football abilities.
These roses are a dark
   deep red.
     Initial reports said Joe'd been
      shot in the head
I remember him; he beat out
  Terry Bradshaw their first year.
     but the hospital later changed
      the report

He didn't last, though;
    wasn't he on drugs?
          and the injury won't hurt his
             football abilities.
I'm really proud of how
    these flowers look.
        "There was some beating of the
          head with a blunt instrument,
But everybody will be
        with a head injury we don't take
             chances,"
watching Bradshaw and the
    Steelers on TV.
        said the head of the shock trauma
            unit,
Don't the roses and
    chrysanthemums look beautiful?
        "but the injury won't hurt his
          football abilities."

THE POEM ABOUT THE
SILLY DREAMERS

The silly dreamers say,
"Now, Loren, let it all
hang out; now really
fantasize. If you could
have whatever woman and
whatever kind of love
you want, who would she
and what would it be?"
The silly dreamers wait,
expecting me to say –
hell, I don't know: Raquel
or Ronstadt, satin sheets
and SuperSex. They wait;
and Loren smiles. And smiles.
Because, my love, you go so
far beyond their silly
fantasies. You give me more
love, more exciting and
more true, than all the
silly dreamers who have ever
dreamed, and all the silly
dreamers who will ever
dream (laid end to end)
could fantasize.

SOMETHING

Something
pressed against these
windows listening to
every note of music
as our records turn.

Something
moved by music but
drawn here as silently
as day and darkness
fill this courtyard
with their alternating
mysteries.

Something
that hears songs on
our records that we
seldom hear unless we
play them over after
love.

Something
from outside that hums
the melodies our ears
missed as we whispered
love three songs or four
or five ago.

JUGGLER

I saw an ad –
comic instruction
book, *Juggling*
for the Absolute
Klutz – and thought
of how adroitly
you can sometimes
juggle
my complexities:
needs
notions
moods
"tensities":
how unaware I am
of being juggled,
except the pleasing
ease of being
three
or
four
small
spheres
that dance up from
and whirl above
your so unklutzy
fingertips.

PART II(A)* REVISITED

In life as in

literature, a

close relationship

may exist between

two persons for a

reason such as the

following: the

persons love to

move together

under budding

limbs, luxuriate

near pink

white

golden petals; the

persons, apart,

feel empty

hollow

half-alive, hunger

for each other;

the persons feel a

magic thrill as

tips of bodies

touch, a wondrous

warmth as fluids

blend; or, the

persons, after

loving, glow with

health

vitality,

feel wholly satis-

fied

fulfilled.

From the true life

experiences you

have had, choose a

total of *two*. In

each case briefly

describe the close

relationship between

two persons and by

specific references

show that it exists

for one of the

above reasons.

* Apologies (?) to The
University of the
State of New York
Regents High School
Comprehensive Examination
in English.

GOMER: TO HER
HUSBAND, HOSEA

You're too gentle. I'm
not used to that. You
want love to be – I
don't know – love!
Love is what I make,
man, make to him, and
him, to get my wool,
corn, flax, oil, wine.
And if it feels good
to me once in fifty
times, I'm lucky, like
a waitress with a
generous tip. But you
get to me sometimes,
and I wish I could
feel love, really,
your kind. I think I
did once, for a little
while. It was when our
baby's mouth was pulling
on my nipple, and I had
some kind of mother-
feeling, and knew you
were the father: that
was nice. But after that,
it all went haywire. The
other babies weren't
from you or, worse, I
wasn't sure. And I was
gone a lot with him, or
him, and when I was
here, you were always
listening to some Voice
in the dark, or writing,
writing. You're too

gentle. Even when you
tell me off, you use
words like, "Your
goodness is a morning
cloud; like early dew
it goes away." And one
time you forgot my name;
you called me "Israel."
I just feel very strange
in this house now. I do
appreciate how much you
care; nobody ever did
before. But your love's
wasted on me. Give it to
the children when I'm gone.

WHEN

Not to sound facile
like a greeting card
(clever, clichéd, cute)
but the times I love
you most *are* when I'm
with you and when I'm
not: Cool today, your
sweet hand gliding on
my skin, making my
back turn on and glow;
and muggy last night,
sleepless among twisted
sheets, looking for a
feather-flutter of
your lightest breath.
Mornings you brighten
walking in, your colors
and smile making even
my dishwasher turn on;
and grey strange wakings
wishing you (cliché,
cliché) were here.

LOVE SONG TO A DAUGHTER

for Kathy

This rain strokes us out
of August, strokes us
into autumn, accompanied
by sadness, not profound
but greyer than those cello
notes that sometimes seem
to fill the minutes between
Sunday afternoon and
Monday morning. Caught in
a change of seasons, a
transition from weekend to
week, we lost whole years,
we two, years when you
seemed too old for me to
touch, though it was I whose
mirror slowly filled with
grey. I made awkward gestures,
sent bright cards from out-of-
town, touched other children
who seemed young. Then one
day, on an ageless stairway,
where I thought we both were
thinking more of someone else,
you touched me, and we held,
and things began to change.
Thank you for that. I'd been
so in-between, tried so hard
not to trespass that I'd
misread Welcome signs. September
beckons, telling me again how
good it is to have a daughter
young enough to understand an
awkward father, and forgive
grey strokes of rain.

WE HAVE NOT KNOWN
MUCH OF THE NIGHT

We have not known much
of the night, but most of
what we have shared has been
ecstasy. Our journey out of
Canada – the Q.E.W. – dancing
with three hands, driving with
one. Our thirty minute gap in
Star Wars while we sent soft
stars warm through each other
(other, other). Always a bed,
mostly one that one of us
would have to leave before
the dawn. But we have slept
(really slept) together a few
times: not many hours before we
turned, both wanting love, more
love, much more than sleep.
Whatever we have missed, my
darling, we have shared much sweetness
in the fragmentary moments
we have known of night.

DO YOU?

I don't know
yet what you
want from me,
do you? I think
you want to
keep my anger
on a stage,
my sadness in
a book, keep
us light, laughing.
I love to
laugh, lie on
your floor with
you, and laugh.
Is that what
I should give,
you get? I
don't know yet
what, do you?

MOSTLY LIGHT

We saw, and felt, a special
light throughout the film
(The light of Northern Italy,
you said, caresses, like the
language). It softened peasants'
cheekbones, gave their poverty the
pale glow faith might hope to give.

There was a special light in
your half-moved-into apartment
too, soft, pleasant, even if the
lamp belonged, like the peasants'
gentle animals, to the padrone.

We caressed soft cheeks, matched
each other's gentleness, felt warm
light spread inside. You nestled
into sleep, breathing in the
silence like a fresh green plant.

The dark struck soon, struck me
with rattle of wrong stair, wrong
door, scared you awake. An awkward
lovely start for us: a little
sudden dark, but mostly light.

MIDNIGHT: ELLICOTT CREEK ROAD

Driving slowly, street

        slick with wet leaves,

rain still falling

        just enough to need

the wipers on, pleasantly

        relaxed, tired

        just enough to ease

right into sleep at home.

Radio guitar notes strumming me,

sure that you're almost asleep by

now, happy,

        (relaxed, like me,)

Once home, I'll dial your

        number, let it ring

once,

        just enough to let

you know.

DIED

Othello died still acting,
singing, dancing. Died dancing.

Othello had a heart
attack, died, acting, not
in Act Five but,
like Caesar, in
Act Three,
much left to do.

(Letters of eight years
ago or more begin to
come back; bits of, words
from, phrase recall. He
stands before me as he
didn't then, dances Othello
on a stage so tiny there is
barely room for Desdemona,
tups her in locked chambers,
her shadow pale, his forked
dark form impaling hers)

Othello suffered cardiac arrest,
died singing, not the closing
aria, but
earlier recitative.

Othello died still acting,
singing, dancing. Died dancing.

IN MEMORY OF
KATHY SKONEY

1

I've sought her
in unlikely places
this October afternoon.
There's Kathy, there,
on that tree branch,
an empty place a
leaf should cling.
I know her perky
tilt, her jaunty grace,
"shaved" head above
brave smile. But
silence isn't like her:
"Chirp, bird, so I'm
sure it's you." She
taught me one can
almost always smile;
I try hard not to
cry. I blink, and
look for Kathy, and I
see an empty place
a leaf should cling.

2

All I know of where
she is, is it's an
older world than ours,
more whole, and people
there are finished and
complete, with qualities
we've lost, or never
had. I've sought her
in unlikely places. In
some deeper permanence
she smiles. If
there are angels, they
stand silent, awed.

BRIDGE-CENTER

Now we meet, at last,
here at bridge-center,
our river batters the
abutments, our magical
antennae touch, and
hold, and form again,
our bridge. Remember
how you started from
your bridge-end, I
from mine? How each
felt nerve-ends barely
touch, move lightly,
felt the other start
to move onto the
the bridge, the bridge
itself begin to form,
to be, to gently press,
rotate, connect us with
the lightning that
would weld the firm
ecstatic silver-pink
strong arching rain-
bow of the bridge?

WILDFLOWER MUSIC

Edging streets,
driveways, and
parking lots, blue
white gold clarinets
of chicory, Queen
Anne's lace, and
tall dandelions.

Half-hidden, tiger
lilies, brassy
sweet a month ago,
part of the garden's
world now, not
the field's: a
muted orange choir.

Along the highway,
whole symphonies of
loosestrife, the
morning sun upbowing
all the flowers'
purple, downbowing all
the grasses' green.

MOMENT FOR A GESTURE

"There is no shining disc
climbing upward. There is
no noble pine to shelter me.
Nor is there a sparkling sea."
                    - Mishima

The moment, when it

comes, won't be dramatic,

will it? Is any moment

ever? Except with the

momentous momentary

drama we ourselves inject.

Someone will mutter

"Boring," probably;

someone will yawn. Or

it will be too far

from a service area,

or too near home.

We've passed the last

Thanksgiving, not long

until the final Christmas:

this decade has decayed

like long-neglected teeth.

The New Year wants to
be ten new years,
each one novocained,
drilled, filled with
days of undramatic moments,

one no better or no
worse than any other.
Wait right here a moment,
while I go and make
this gesture. Probably,
I'll be right back.

AWAY

They walked by a river,
hand in hand, too cold
to take off gloves. Snow
fell, expected, the good
weather gone. They walked
in shadows near a river,
heavy after a snowstorm.
They paused to consider
possibilities, to play on
keys, on strings, of
feeling. They would never
fall in love again. Not
like the first time. They
walked away from more than
snowdrifts on a riverbank.

TERRY FOX

The early-morning
road belongs to
him. He tapped his
name forever on its
shoulder: Terry Fox
Terry Fox Terry
Fox. The thread of
sunlight slips into
the eye of darkness.
Day lilies unfold
orange petals. The
brave one-legged
runner's dead of
cancer. The chicory
along the road is
luminously blue. The
hop-skip of his
weary steps still
taps his name: Terry
Fox Terry Fox Terry
Fox

TEN A.M. SATURDAY DECEMBER 6

I like the way blue flames
climb clinging to the roundness
of our copper water kettle
When I turn the heat down
slightly one blue tongue
still lightly licks
the copper surface
Coffee from our kettle
keeps a flamey feeling
black and hot in my
green-handled coffee mug

I should go in and watch
you sleep   I like to do that
but it's good to sit here
sipping coffee slowly
(Saturday is lazy time)
and knowing you are warm
and happy under soft blue
blankets clinging to your
rounded softness like blue
flames that flicker lightly
round your body in our bed

I DON'T WANT TO HEAR IT

Yes, I still have the
record: I don't want
to hear it. And I'm
not sure why. I loved the
passages for solo piano
as much as any music I
have ever heard: I used
to go to sleep savoring
its soft familiarity.
I knew exactly where the
changes came, the pauses,
where the strongest of the
melodies emerged from the
weave, the tributaries
became the main stream. I
always was awake, just
still awake, when that
theme began. And I would
never hear it end. Sleep
wove itself each night
into that melody, I never
felt it happen, it just
did. I held the record in
my hands today. It's very

worn: but that's not why
I didn't play it. I sleep
to other music or no music
now. Maybe I think it
would be disappointing:
there's a good chance
that it would, and not
because of wornness,
scratchiness. Maybe I
think it would bring
people back, associations,
from that time: no doubt
it would do that, too.
I just don't want to
play it, hear it. Anytime.
Especially when I lie
down to try to sleep.

FLOAT

On clear water

in bowls the

color of canary

feathers, float

(like yellow

      flames)

chrysanthemums.

PEEL OFF MY FACE

Peel off my face:
another face beneath.
You've glimpsed it,
but you ought to
really see it.
Peel off the kind,
the bright, expressive,
strong: the actor's
face, the writer's,
lover's. Get down to
my other face: so sad,
blank, animal: face
of a man (no matter
if my words pour silver,
foaming, filling all
the golden steins of
silence) – a man with
no words, with no
words, for what I
sometimes feel.

TRUE

She asked to sing
songs she could feel
"so the people
feel them too"
                songs
about "the mourner
in the corner
                first
they break you then
forsake you"
                love
laments   booze blues
trite and true
                True
was where she walked
from
spoke true sang true
knew the pushers of
the lies would
break her
of her one good habit
                lonely
mourner in the corner
even under hot lamps
                high
up there in the spot
glare
belting with heavy
amps
forsaken   breakin'
feels the songs so
        strong that
she can't sing

HAZY LIGHT

No snow

cover, hover

of dove

haze, day's

pale ale

light, night

gone, dawn

near, here.

LEAN

That   warm   night

my   body   lay

with   empty   arms

dreaming   of   you.

My   house   was

lean   and   troubled.

My   fingers   turned

the   fragile   pages

of   remembered   joy,

reached   out   to

fondle   the   long

petals   of   your

glowing   absence.

WE'VE LEARNED TO
UNDERSTAND

You and I have
learned (the better
we know each other,
the better we know
ourselves, the more
there is to know)
to understand some
other people who
don't understand
anyone, especially
themselves, who
keep intruding on
our lives as if
they had our good
in mind instead of
just always their own.

COMBINATION

A flute is
playing clear
melodic lilting
sounds above a
cushion of cello
notes. Outside
my window, early
evening is as dark
as midnight, but
the snow gleams
up from the ground
to light things a
little. I'm not
waiting, exactly,
just wondering if
you might call in
these few minutes
just before I leave.
I feel such love
for you, a combination
of the clarity and
lilt and melody the
flute is singing and
the snowgleam in the
early darkness, that
kind of quiet, soft,
bright love. If you
just let it, it will
float in through your
window, and we'll hold
it (there and here)
together in our hands.

WOULDN'T LET IT BE

The day would

have been warm

We wouldn't

let it be

Like birds from

behind bars

we kept watching

the ocean freeze

No communication

except through

silences and

there were not

enough

None of us would

let the day

be warm

SPRING

The season is

significant.

Your hand's a

feather in my

grass. I flower

on your branch.

Snow ghosts are

stillborn. We

have brought

spring

to the world.

DAY LILIES EXIT,
ENTER LOOSESTRIFE

Day lilies exit,

enter loosestrife:

happen in one

morning or just

seem to? Mid-July,

no fanfare, one

morning disappear

the orange trumpets,

purple spikes rise

filling fields.

GREENGOLD

Gold rising from green –
gold illumined from
within in absence of
electric light, mums
glowing palely yellow –
my God! – light directly
overhead infolds unfolds
their gold, green stems
reach down to water in
this green glass vase,
these multi-petaled
flowers settle, multi-
karat jewels, ring above
this ring of green clear
water, golden brilliants
fill this green glass
vase with rising light.

GREYING

one greyish

songbird

fluting spring

feeling   One

greyish crocus

flaunting

spring fashion

One greying

snowman

thwarting spring

thaw   One

greying lover

thinking

spring thought

MINIATURE

Lights like silver
needles   One tiny
dancer pirouettes
Tiny bows glide
over strings of
tiny cellos   One
dancer pirouettes
Hands out in the
concert hall
applaud   Hands
reach out from the
audience with roses
Silver needles thread
themselves with
darkness   One tiny
dancer dreams   In a
corner in the morning
of the dream two
tiny dancing slippers
nestle among roses

FOREHEADS

Clear the grey

clouds from the

face of the

white-silver moon:

draw the horizon

between the white

sky and grey

ocean: surround

the grey rocks

with white flowers

so tall that

they cling to the

foreheads of stars.

SNOWFLAKES IN OCTOBER

(after Burchfield)

Snowflakes in October

drift, float; leaves

maneuver, turn. flakes

glide; leaves pirouette.

ease more, fret less.

white, soft; not orange,

brittle. salt the sky,

not speckle.

MY OUTER TREES

These thickets of pine

give way, those fields

widen into treeless

marshplains growing toward

the shore, where a few

last trees, my outer trees,

trees with the roar of the waves

in their leaves, lean toward the sea,

homesick for saltspray, lonely

for seasound, as I am today

elbows deep in needles

here beneath this forest pine.

FATHER/SON HEAVEN

I see it as a fishing
place: there I am with
my father in a boat. He
doesn't make fun of the
way I put worms on the
hooks; I'm not uptight
about impressing him.
We both relax and let
the sunset seep into
our bodies, let the
gentle waves from other
boats lap at our oars,
and let the peaceful
darkness settle on our
shoulders: *ours*, on his,
on mine; with some soft
and forgiving mutuality.

DREAM

for Chick Corea

Not my dream, yours,
not one I wake from
or react to, not one
I interpret, nor one
like any I
have had. A thick, a
tense dream, yours,
tightrope through a
fog, a narrow tunnel,
no light at the end.
Yet how it sings, it
flows, your dream,
through weighted dark
through giant snowballs
made of hard-packed
silence, not a sharp
knife slicing cheese or
bread, no, more like
footprints that you know
go clear across the
field, the wide white
field, in spite of all
the snow that's fallen
since, that's covered
those footprints. No
matter, you still know
so well they're there.

THE DREAM ABOUT YOU

One thing, especially,
was different from any
dream, or kind of dream,
I've had: I knew, right
in the middle of it, that
I didn't want to wake up.
You know, sometimes you
wake, and wish you hadn't,
and hope you can go back
to sleep and right back
into it. But I knew, this
time, this dream, that I
wanted it to go on, go on,
never (you know?), never
end. There wasn't really
that much to it. You were
stretched out on the floor,
in some position Dr. Tucker
recommends. And I was next
to you. And I reached over
-- no, wait – what made it
sweet was that we both
reached over at the same
amazing moment and – it
sounds a little adolescent,
but it wasn't, not at all –
we very gently held each
other's hand. And I tried
to say something, so did
you. But we decided that
our hands had said it all.

TWO PAINTINGS BY MILTON AVERY

I. Tangerine Moon and Wine Dark Sea

take a horizon

three horizontal

parallels: a

coral sky   a

rick rack shore

a large oblong

of sea   now

take a moon –

a wedge of its

fruit cut away

-- and tilt it

in the sky

just resting

tangerinely on

the shore

II. Dark Forest

the dust-beige

country road

will always

disappear

down the hill

it has always

just climbed the

other side of

between the

brownish fields

it disappears

into the dark

green forest

and the dark

aqua sky

THE ROWBOAT DREAM

Lately the place I
count on seeing you
is in dreams like the
rowboat one: I'm rowing
carefully, no klutzy
strokes, a smooth ride
in calm water. I know
we'll get there safely,
and you'll have a good
chance to relax. My
only worry (in the
dream) is that you
might prefer more
speed, somebody else's
motorboat. Not that you
say that, I just worry.
It's night, the sky is
dark gray velvet, really
velvet when I reach my
fingers up and touch.
You can't quite reach,
I'm taller, but you
take my word for the
sky's texture. And then
(you know how dreams are)
I'm touching you, and
you're more velvet than
the sky. And I row
smoothly, and we get
there, or we're just
about to, when I wake.

REACHING

all my fingertips

kept trying to touch

stars last night

until this morning

when the same stars

fell into my hands

like drops of rain

and this afternoon

I didn't see it

but I know the rain

was drawn back up

to blue pools that

are black tonight

and all my finger-

tips keep reaching

toward the liquid

light of stars

WIND AND DREAM

The wind's a grey wolf

beyond windows wailing

for a mate, an abused

brother begging keepers

for release. This fear

that night unleashes

preys on wind's grey

bier, pulls the last

rug from under easy

knees, rolls inside a

cozy carpet of a dream

of love, wall-to-wall

and warm away from wind.

IN MEMORY OF PANCHO

Old Panch was
a child who had
grown very old
but never stopped
being a child.

The fireplace
misses him.
The firelight
searches through
the room and
doesn't find him.

Degrees of
comparison: rather
old, very old;
pretty old, beautiful
old. Panch was pretty
homely, but beautiful
homely too.

Even when we
laughed at him,
it came out
warm and sad.

He taught us things by
being them. The weary
aching bulky little
body that he dragged
around, half blind, on
less than four good
feet, embodied patience,
love, endurance. Pancho
taught us those. We
were slow learners,

but we learned.

The fireplace misses
him. The firelight
searches
through the room and
doesn't find him.

Innocent to the last:
One of us
held him,
the vet gave him the
gentle needle. Panch
died innocent as rain,
older than heaven,
still a child.

(BATH, TEA, ROBE, BED)

We made (bath, tea,

robe, bed) a cold

day warm. Your

thoughts, you

thought, were too

much, many, to

allow for sleep.

You slept, and I

slept with you. Or

we walked above a

mountain path (bath,

tea, robe, bed)

awake, asleep, and

you are still inside

me inside you.

NEW

Everything seemed

new and special,

from the ordinary

sidewalk (near my

door) which I had

never used, to the

extraordinary sweet

long silences we

breathed together,

very late that night

but very early in

this new and special

year.

FROM THE SEA

for "Ida"

This is a letter
from the sea. It's
not in rhyme. It
could be. Should
it be? Don't only
songs rhyme? And
then in case of
wrongs, when
serious mistakes
are made? Letters
can't be mailed to
outside over there.
And they're sometimes
so late, when sent to
right side round,
that the solution has
been found, and all
the words are déja
vu, the nightmare
all lived through.
This is a late and
unrhymed letter
from the sea.

(Based on Maurice Sendak's
Outside Over There)

HAPPY NEED

Three years ago we
started with "You
Needed Me." Each of
us is happy these
days, making people
into books and
memories for people.
It's less easy, at
a happy time, to
need. Happy puts on
tinted glasses,
travels incognito,
whispers "I'm OK
alone." But Happy
also needs to borrow
warm socks and share
lemon tea. We still
need each other…
What we have is
lovely, and it helps
us understand that
happiness is quite
compatible with need.

NIGHT

A single stone

at the bottom

of black water.

A memory of

honey poured.

The stillness

between chirps

of insects.

The dark sky

between stars.

A night to

stretch out the

north over the

empty place.

A night to

hang the earth

upon nothing.

LISTENING TO BRUCH'S
KOL NIDREI

for Robyn

Barely autumn, but

it has been years

since summer. The

clouds all week:

low, heavy, grey.

People breathe out

air in puffs, like

smoke. The cello

prays, sorrowfully,

with five days left

till Yom Kippur. The

world needs more than

one Day of Atonement.

But it's right the one,

this year, comes during

this dark time. Bruch

was not a Jew, and I'm

not. Being human, sad,

may matter more. The

cello repeats all the

vows, breath almost visible.

SHOULD BE

There should be

a song   there

is a song   not

everyone can sing

it   I can't

right now   a song

that "tells it,

you know, like it

is"   It isn't

possible   right

now   to know the

way it is, let

alone tell it   to

sing it   totally

impossible   so the

song there is   is

useless   empty

and I'm left   repeating

"there should be a

song a song a song"

BREAK

We took a love

break from a mad

world, and hid

from assassins of

peace. We picked

stars and flowers

in our sky-high

meadow, picked

flowers and stars.

Then,

hands full of pink

star-shaped roses,

arms spangled with

daisy-shaped stars,

we wandered back

down to a world that

has murdered Sadat.

Hostage

for Bill Goss

One

Fear is the constant,
but subdued, to varying
degrees. Night is no
easier than ever, sleep
no erasure, morning never
a fresh start. A sense of
important cheerful messages,
tapped on the far side of
impenetrable walls. The
problem Brodsky felt in
first exile, of "how to
change the pace of a man's
life – slowing from run
to walk – without breaking
the rhythm of his breath."
Fear is the constant, but
with boredom somehow also
flowing through fear's veins.

Two

(Help me.) You know we
will repeatedly refuse
to accede to the terrorists'
demands. (Help me.) Don't
be antagonistic nor subservient.
Just be yourself: enduring
will be made a little easier.
(Help me.) The worst is over
after 48 hours. The danger
doesn't disappear but it
declines from there. (Help
me.) Terrorists, too, feel
isolated, surrounded, feel
lots of other pressures.
(Help me.) Time is on our
side. Just give us time,
have patience; we will work
a peaceful resolution. (Help

Three

A changeable, strange season:
calendar winter, but often
looks, feels, like any of the
other three.

A season for insistence on
release of hostages: white
armbands, patriotic pledges,
fierce graffiti.

The winter of our malcontents
who fire their darts at Aya-
tollah boards and murmur
"hostage" as their new Amen.

Are we making hostages our
gods? Or (Rukeyser): "God
reduced to a hostage
among hostages*"?

Pathetic or indifferent,
this season too will pass.
Khomeini will be just a foreign
word again, like Tanya, or like oil.

Still it must be hard, ironic,
to be Patty Hearst, watching us
go hostage-happy in the decade
she was jailed for being one.

* 1944!

Four

(after Cummings/Dostoevsky/Solzhenitsyn)

If finally I make my exit,
the part of me referred to
as my "mind" will still be
slightly bent and twisted.
The hours before my some-
what supernatural departure
into freedom I'll attempt
to straighten myself out.

My dreams and long removal
from reality make me think
freedom's somehow freer
than it really is. It's
natural for any hostage to
exaggerate where freedom is
concerned.

They'll change
the rules any way they want.
They'll never let me go. But
sometimes I get feeling way
inside, "God, just think, one
day I might walk out, go home."
So I just go on living like
this, my eyes on the floor,
trying not to think of why I'm
here, or whether I'll get out.

Five

There was nothing
left to hang on to
but missing. Miss
something: that was
vital. I made bad
inner jokes, like
"Miss America?" but
this was not a joke.
Miss something: cling
to an empty space.
I did. I concen-
trated on it, missed
it, although I
never quite knew
what it was.

Six

(Released because of illness
diagnosed as sclerosis, he
sits in a wheelchair at home.
He has been reading Byron's
The Prisoner of Chillon.)

"My limbs are bow'd,
though not with toil,
but rusted with a
vile repose." Not
rusted, either,
like iron, not
lignified to oak. My
body will petrify
slowly, sclerose,
into a stony replica
of that dank basement
-- I called it The
Tomb – near total
darkness, no fresh
air.

"A kind of change
came in my fate."
They blindfolded me and
moved me to another
building where the
windows had been sealed.
Intense excitement when
day broke! "I saw the
glimmer of the sun
creeping as it before
had done." A glimpse
of light between

two bricks of
those sclerotic walls.
Excitement
went away. "Among
the stones I
stood a stone."

"A light broke in
upon my brain." I
heard two voices:
young girls talking
in the street
beyond the wall,
walking to
school, I guess.

Light and voices
went away. "It might
be months, or years,
or days, I kept no
count, I took no
note…
At last
men came to set me
free." Free. To
become a statue, The
Hostage Monument,
flesh metamorphosed
slowly into
standing stone.

Seven

Fantasy of rescue:
Fifty-two red white
blue choppers drop
in cotton silence,
rise, each with one
hostage passenger.

Nightmare: Choppers
drive around the
ground, bump like
Dodgems, smash
like demo derbies!

Fantasy: Fifty-two
red white blue
camels trek through
trackless sand and
back, each bearing
one hostage back to
Jefferson.
Or Carter.
Almost any President.

Eight

Lame duck excess/
grim revelation/
confetti snow on
yellow-ribboned trees/
legit gripes of abused
Viet vets/ video senti-
ment orgies/ blame/
praise

Is it enough to be a
former hostage –
"out of there"?
Shouldn't it mean
something, signify…?
After boredom, fear,
"Help me," doubts,
never feeling free,
turned to stone,
dreaming rescue –

FLASH! montage of
sudden interview,
speech, spotlight,
emerge as…myself?
The world needs categories,
labels: Hostage, Former.
          Ribbon, Yellow.
          Symbol, Liberation.
          Hero-Martyr.
Worth it? I don't think
it made sense or was
worth it: And it's an
anticlimax re-becoming
what I was before.

MANON

for Barb

"My fingers closed on the fingers of a
little ice-cold hand! The intense horror
of nightmare came over me: I tried to
draw back my arm, but the hand clung to
it, and a most melancholy voice sobbed,
'Let me in – let me in!'… As it spoke
I discerned obscurely a child's face
looking through the window."

- Wuthering Heights

She is cool rainfall
on a summer beach. She
is a fingernail rasped
across a chalkboard.
Thirteen. In love so
with her mother that
she hurts her with it:
"I'll kidnap you and
steal for you, we'll
die together, our blood
will mingle on the
pavement, from it will
grow a flower that
cannot be crushed."

Hates everyone her
mother cares about:
the gross drunk moron
brother, the siren-
happy cop boyfriend.
Does fast cars until
speed scares, does
truancies, fantasies.
In all her lonely
times she reads: heights

392

wuthered by nightmare and
passion, sad storms,
laughing gales. Reality
intrudes – men paw
her mother's flesh.

Little kid woman
walking the roads in
her jeans. Thirteen,
with roots in the blood
on the pavement, growing
up from it, love flower
hate weed that cannot
be crushed, face in the
rain, fingernails on
cold windows, voice
rasping, "You! Let me in!"

Based on the central
character in the film
Les Bons Debarras

"MUST"

Playing "pretend" when
you were kids, did you
use the word "must" the
charming way we did?
"You must be the mother,
and I must be the father,
and you've been at work,
even though it's Saturday,
so I must surprise you
by cooking dinner. Let's
see, I must make chicken
livers in gravy, with
broccoli and mushrooms,
and I must serve it to
you over rice. And after-
wards we must go to bed
and love each other as
a good mother and father
would." Mustn't we?

YOU ARE

You are (how in

this world, these

words, can I

express it?) – you

are the constant

presence in the

center of me that

the rest revolve

around. You are

the silent impulse

in my heart that

causes it to beat

the next heartbeat,

the next; the secret

urging in my lungs

to breathe, to

breathe.

RENEWAL

I have bright flowers
on my table this third
day of our third
November. Outside
the windows, our
third winter darkens
its gathering skies,
prepares to powder
our warm coats with
snow, tomorrow, or
tomorrow. I look out,
remember yesterday,
here, in our warm
bodies, we renewed
our love. Our yester-
days have all been
lighted with bright
flowers: with yellow
mums, with pink
carnations. It was
sweet to rise from
love's renewal,
still feeling new
warm flowers springing
from our touching flesh,
and find fresh flowers
on the table, as they've
always been. I gave you
some to light your way,
and I still have more
pink and yellow
flowers on my table
this third day of
our third November.

AFTER MISREADING ONE WORD
IN ELIZABETH BISHOP'S
"NORTH HAVEN"

The poem Bishop wrote
when Lowell died
lamented his endless
revisions' end:
"You can't derange,
or re-arrange,/
your poems again"
she wrote. And I
misread one word
in the parentheses
that followed: "(But
the Sparrows scan
their song)" I read.
And conjured visions
of his influence on
songbirds, causing
them to re-do songs
(as he re-did and
re-did poems),
scanning them with
sparrow-eyes and
bird brains, to
improve, some Lowell
how, on Nature.
The word was not
"scan," I found
later, only "can."
But I like my first
vision. This time
I will not revise.

COLD FEET

My July sunburn
reminds me of your
spring (Florida)
sunburn, the toucher
careful in touching,
cautious of hurting,
the touchee eager for
loving, even if it
hurts. This heat
today reminds me
spring was cold. You
(back from Florida),
before you slipped
your reddened body
into bed, warmed
your feet in water
in that special way,
prompting my enthus-
iastic "nice to
have your feet
back in my sink!"

BEGINNING

Kathy and Bruce
August 16, 1980

I picture dawn, a hillside
sloping to a lake. You sit
together in still dark
grass, watching the sun ease
from beneath the lavender
cloud blanket, sun softly
edging with orange the oval
lilac lake. Slowly the sky
pales to off-white, soft
blue. Silver rises from the
dew-bright grass, meets sky
gold flowing down. You walk
together up the hill, sharing
the many colors of beginning.

THE MOMENT

The moment we
know well, yet
do not know at
all, the moment
deep within the
soft exploding
flower of each
other, deep beyond
all ordinary
knowledge, beyond
music, memory, and
consciousness, in
the deep pulsating
heart of everything,
the moment we lose
our selves and come
into some new and
ancient kind of
knowledge: knowing
you that moment
become me
becoming you.

PEACE AND LOVE

You lie beside me
peacefully asleep.
You glow with love.
How few times –
nine or ten? –
I've ever seen you
sleeping. I draw a
careful breath and
watch you breathe.
I know how tired
you are. Almost,
I could regret I
woke you earlier, my
fingers trembling
toward your clefts
and tips to nibble,
stroke. Almost, I
could be sad I
woke you from a
sleep so peaceful
-- even for that,
even for our coming
glow. Peace and
love are both so
scarce and precious
in the world: how
good to know I
didn't really have
to choose between.

ASTURIAS

An idiot takes
broken-legged
leaps from one
volcano to
another, sky to
sky, lip torn,
lids burning,
labyrinth inside
his bones,
beneath the
lightning flashes
in the blood-red
skies. A woman,
sold, hugs her
dead baby,
stinking, till
whores bury it,
white satin
lines the coffin.
A heart, a star,
Camila loves
Miguel, a crown
of thorns: graffiti
on walls. The
presidential
darkness swallows
walls like wafers,
drinks the cup of
sacramental
excrement.

SIR: AN OPEN LETTER
TO SAINT PETER

Sir, this will introduce
our gentle friend Bill
Walter. He's a little
early for his date with
you. But he was late
for everything down
here. Not careless or
disorganized; he just
took time with each
connection
and so was late
the next one. He concen-
trated when he talked,
listened; we were
the only person, only
matter, on his mind. He
gave us his attention
and his time.
Sir, we know that you
aren't sitting at some
Pearlgate
asking questions
of the ones of us who get
that far. But, uh, just in case
you are, this will introduce
our friend Bill Walter.
Ask him
what you please,
you'll like his answers.
You'll enjoy the conver-
sation. And eternity
should be just long enough.

The Skier
and the Snow

for
Michael Sneath 1952-1977

The sky is black
but here and here
where the drifts slope
slant just right
starlight reflects
dimly from the snow
Soon sharp cold stars
pierce singly through
the blackness: chilled
laser beams of light
Our fragile human dreams
sift down like snowflakes
Skiers silent as angels
wing down spotless
mountainsides of winter
white teeth clear eyes
lungs breathing in
the cleaner cleanest
mountain air

It is the skier's

last night on the slope

He doesn't know

One night seems like another

only good conditions

fair conditions

There are things

which make one night stand out

But they are mostly inner things

some feel

       some knowledge

that the body will be right

will do things this night

it could never do before

but nothing's really special

about the last night

unless you know it is the last

He doesn't know

I've hated snow
and lived in Buffalo
for forty-seven years
There have been times
I guess
I've loved snow too
Runny-nosed little Loren
played on "mountains"
coming home from school
Once very young he lay down
in a field of snow
and fell asleep
I must have loved it then
and I remember driving
through snow with a
special person once
through flakes so large
they brushed and there was
hardly room for sky between
past trees puffed into giant
mushrooms gorgeous white
Of course I loved snow
when my children loved it
played in it with me
til we all got wet and cold
and went to get hot chocolate
and warm

But hated too

Childhood snow nostalgia fades

We hate these piles of white

we can't control

Snow hits us like a paralytic stroke

chokes highway arteries

blocks trains

     grounds airplanes

        fells power lines

           breaks bodies

              smashes cars

Snow mounts up to the eaves of houses

like the bad old days

when horse-hauled sleighs

were galloped over drifts

at treetop heights

and "the car stalls,

Churning in a snowdrift…"

The skier is

the last one

on the slope tonight

He knows

or thinks he knows

he is alone

stands poised

a powder of snow blown over him

pure white

The snow continues

fountains over him

makes a fine glittering mist

here in the pale surrounding light

Pushing in his slender poles

he slides away

down the gradual slope

The hushed and only

sound is this quick

dreamlike windrush of his skis

snow

gleaming on a woman's lashes

on a winter night

snow-muffled silence

in deep woods

soaked snowsuits

skinned from kids

a snow-filled driveway

shoveled clean just as

a plow comes by and

piles the entrance high again

students

and their teachers

listening to

early morning radios

hoping school is closed

because of snow

Star-eager voyagers who arc

out into deeper space

will see one last light

from the earth:

the light from polar snow

Look closely at this snowflake

see its special beauty

realize each snowflake

that has fallen throughout time

that will fall through

what still remains of time

is unique like this one in

symmetry and mystery and form

The helplessness: a gust
spins me forward several yards
and plunges me in this dense
whirl of drift Breathless and
dazed snow in my mouth inside
my collar up my sleeves I try
to stand Another gust hurls
itself at my face cuts off
my breath again
and for an awful second
I believe the storm knows I
am here is focusing its
force on me I panic thrash out
with my arms I stumble back
and flop here on my back
arms spread across this drift

Earth beneath snow

has its own flow of warmth

a little like the blood flow under skin

The snow protects the flow

sustains the warmth

The life beneath will never freeze

layer by layer to its core

People live beneath snow

live inside shelters built of snow

Snow is a living substance you can ride upon

can tunnel through

      feel touch you gently

        whip and sting you

          melt or freeze

awesomely ugly

      or majestically beautiful

For George and Beth

"I have been preoccupied with the thought of fundamental man. Man identical with himself from the earliest civilizations; identical with the townsmen of Babylon. Identical with the semi-gorilla who, lifting up his eyes, for the first time felt himself one with the star-studded sky…Identical with so many dead…more dead than living"

- Andre Malraux, *Lazarus*

The skier stands poised for his final run

aware of earth beneath snow

beneath skis

       beneath feet

aware he stands on some portion

of earth surface

wonders what if this snow were bottomless

what if instead of standing on a firm hilltop

he now was falling endlessly

past clouds

like snow through snow

falling as snow always falls

fragile soft and steadily

Years pass and decades pass and centuries

and still the snow falls

The skier stands at the head of the slope

looks up and finds himself one with the stars

looks down and finds himself one with the snow

pushes with his poles

and glides on down the slope

behind him ski tracks slowly fill with snow

We will listen always to the lovely

windrush of his skis.

As I Might
Hold A Bird

for Kathy

for Jim

for Bob

for Barb

WHEN THEY FLEW AWAY

Many birds: tiny, and
black from here: rising
suddenly from the same
tree and scattering off
into small bushes all
over the meadow. He has
just begun to notice
birds, to really see
them, after years of
thinking he was looking
at them. Is there a way
to put a world back
together? It isn't like
a puzzle, cut precisely
by a jigsaw, fragmented
in a pattern, the pieces
cut to fit each to each,
together, back into the
whole. No, when a world
explodes, some pieces are
destroyed forever, or
mutilated beyond recognition.
And some are like those

birds: scattered suddenly
into new places, new
surroundings. And he
doesn't know how they
were arranged in that
first tree. He never
looked closely enough
at them. He only started
to notice them when they
flew away in all directions.
He can wander through the
wreckage, picking up
tiny pieces of his world,
holding them in his hands
as he might hold a bird,
to know it in a way he
never did before: the
warmth and tremble of it,
the needing to be free,
the shivering awareness
of minuteness, fragility,
mortality.

WALKS DOWN LIGHTED STREETS

He was not known in
that place, and used
to take long walks at
night down lighted
streets with trees. He
lived quite near the
park, and often walked
across it near the zoo,
hearing the sounds of
sad caged animals
trying to learn to
sleep. He left food
in the park sometimes,
on a lone picnic bench
the moon slid grey
across, because a torn
and hungry man came
there most mornings
and would eat if there
was food. When there was
nothing there, the man
would sit all morning
shivering in May or
August. He seldom spoke

to anyone he met on
walks: often there were
two together and they
had their world, or
one man or one woman
hurrying toward the
dawn who might have
been afraid if he had
spoken. But there were
nights when someone
noticed kindness in
his face as he passed
under lights, and came
to him, and those few
people he would touch.

THE STRANGEST

Some nights are stranger
than others. Tonight I
slept two hours right
after dinner and woke to
find things strange. I
want to tell about a man
you never heard of, or
whom you've forgotten. A
man you saw once on the
subway in New York, or
along a street in
Stockholm, Buffalo, or
Rome. A man who visited
your memory because of
his intensity, the
sorrow that you breathed
in from his countenance,
that made you want to
stop and say, "Hey, man,
things just can't be
that bad!" But of course
you never said it,
because you knew intuitively
there was too much to this

man to blunder in upon his
fiercest meditation in
that meddling way. And so
you let him pass into the
autumn valleys where your
memory sheds brilliant
drying leaves, and maybe
hoped that you might see
him sometime, once, again.
But I think secretly you
hoped to lose him in the
cluttered attic where you
store the things you really
hope you'll never have to
see again. So hate me,
brother. I am placing him
behind your mirror where
you have to look whenever
you're not satisfied with
what you see. He won't
peer back at you with eyes
like yours; he isn't much
like you. Or me. He's like
familiar music heard at a
strange hour, a twisted

melody you know as well as
your left arm, until you
find it withered in the
strangest night you've
stayed awake through yet.
A melody that changes
every time you ease your
attention, and makes you,
forces you, to be aware, to
know the beauty of a
passage you would fail to
listen to except for
change, except that it is
strange and new, new at
least tonight, when nothing
somehow is familiar. When
your face looks like mine,
or his, and you're afraid
a little, to assume that
you know who you are. You
might not be the watcher
on a night like this, but
watched. You might not be
the one who says (out of
his ordinary normal
breathing world), "Man,

things just can't be
that bad!" You might be
hearing someone say that
about you, to you. And
for the first time realize
that you've been riding
subways, walking streets,
with an expression so
intense, so strong with
sorrow, guilt, that you
need background music to
interpret your mood to a
passerby. On this strange
night I'm writing about
you. him. me. and I don't
know our name. Some
nights, my brother, are
as strange as this.

WITH ROBIN HOOD

He played alone,
not in the
presence of his
enemies, because
alone his fantasies
would turn out
right.

The big kids
would want to
volley real
arrows at him,
discomfort his
narrow shoulders
with a real rod,
a real quarter-
staff.

Alone in the
narrow valley,
he listened for
a distant sounding
of an imagined

horn.

Horn notes sounded
through the valley,
filling slowly
with lithe tall
shadows, bearded,
costumed in green
gauze.

He had no fear,
for Robin Hood was
with him. He'd
gladly, alone
in the shadow-
filled valley, have
died.

YELLOW LEAF PRAYER

To stay yellow

one more day,

even if it

snows, to cling

to this branch

one more day,

even in wind,

in wind, to

watch that one

red leaf across

the road stay

red, stay red

and cling as

long as I.

Amen.

LOOKING FOR ME

I walked out in the
snow this afternoon,
looking for me, but
I wasn't there. It
was a strange place,
strange time, to look
for me: February in
the woods. But when
you miss someone,
you start to think
he might be anywhere.
I'm no winter walker,
I freeze easily, I
didn't look too long.
I found a dead bird
in the snow, frozen
bright red berries,
tufts of dry wheat-
colored grass. And I
found footsteps there
that looked like mine,
but at woods-edge
they stopped,
the way a bird's might
because it flew away.

WOMAN IN A PARKING LOT

Today a woman in a
parking lot asked me
to take a bird off her
car bumper, out of a
little niche by the
headlight where it
had struck the car,
and died. I worked at
removing it gently.
It was still warm.
As I had it almost
cupped in my right
hand, trying to ease
it from where it was
stuck to the metal,
I turned the tiny warm
thing slightly and
saw a slash of bright
red where it must have
first hit. "It might
get a little messy,"
I said quietly. The
woman handed me two
pink tissues, and I

wrapped them in my hand
around the bird and
lifted it away. I
didn't look for blood
or feathers on the
car. I heard the
woman's "Thank you"
from behind me, but
I didn't turn. "Oh,
that's all right,"
I said. I was
already headed across
the parking lot
toward a dark green
receptacle for waste
paper and, I suppose,
dead birds. On the
receptacle, painted
in white letters, was
the word "Please."

Evening
Everything

SLEEP, WOMAN

Sleep, dawn woman, sleep at midnight,

slender woman, formed of sun silvering a treetip,

of dew accumulating in a flower cup,

sleep like a meadow not yet touched by dawn.

Sleep, noon woman, sleep at midnight,

ripe woman, shaped by sun as fruit, as grain

is shaped, golden and joyful, sleep and dream,

run in sunfields, splash in sunstreams.

Sleep, my sunset woman, sleep at midnight,

deep woman (how your crimson waves crashed all

around my lighthouse), lie as still now as

the water near the dark horizon,

sleep till sunrise silvers you again.

THEIR PLAN

my mother at 84

I'm afraid I shall

spoil it. Do they

suppose I will be

satisfied to be so

passive? Satisfied

with such great

contrast? I'm afraid

I'll spoil their plan.

Oh, I admit it doesn't

seem there's any

trouble, any wrong

round here. And if

there were, they'd

surely fix it.

They seem to think I'd

better fold my hands.

I certainly shall

spoil it if I can.

FOUR WAYS NOT TO
APPROACH BEAUTY: AND
THEIR CONSEQUENCES

1. Too closely: It turns

   brown, grows thorns.

2. Too slowly: Each quarter-

   note of it sounds hollow

   in a separate empty hall.

3. Abstractly: It is mere

   veil, or screen, or sieve.

4. Greedily: It begins to

   melt, to drip, and drip.

ELEGY FOR FRED

I didn't see him in the final years, so I don't really know.
Perhaps he slid down to the bottom like an olive dropped in
gin. Perhaps he staggered, missed the railing, and fell down the
steep stone stairway, bruising, battering himself on every lower
step. I don't know. But I doubt any part of it was easy.

I knew him best way back when he was dreaming about
climbing. He could have been a great piano man, a silver-
tongued sportscaster, an MC on a TV game show, a bowler on
the pro tour, the best damn teacher in the world. He had so
many dreams, and they weren't all that crazy. And they weren't
selfish, either: his dreams always included those he loved.

No, what was crazy was the pressure he put on himself because
he wasn't reaching goals, he wasn't climbing to the top, and
then, as time went on, he couldn't get his foot on the next rung,
or even, later, hold on to it with his hand. The MD's told him
he should find less-pressured work, ease off, aim lower; but he
was hooked on dreams of being something very big, of giving
his wife and his kids a gold key to a diamond future. And he
felt closer to it with each bottle he uncorked.

Tomorrow and tomorrow and tomorrow staggered down the
rutted road, and he'd fall on the gleaming rocks and try to pour
himself straight up again. And inside, very far inside, was still
the good man who knew that it was much too late for dreams,
but knew too well how awful life would be without.

SOLILOQUY FOR NABOTH

Guilt by accusation:
a lying witness
said I blasphemed
God and king.
And so I'm judged.
I should have
seen this coming,
should have known that
when the king "requests,"
that that's an order
to obey. I've been
condemned for
saying no. He wants
my vineyard, just
because it's near
his castle, wants
it as a plot
for growing herbs.
My vineyard,
that my father's
father's father
owned. He said
he'd give me, in
return, a "better"
vineyard, or the
"worth of it" in money.
I said, "My God
forbids me to give
you my heritage."
He'll get it, though,
when they have finished
stoning me, and
I am dead.

He's not so bad,
Ahab, as kings go.

He may have sulked
about my saying no,
but I doubt he'd
do this. No, it
must be that queen,
that Jezebel. I
always thought she
wore the royal pants.
She must have
set this trial up,
paid off the witness,
to get rid of me
and give King Hubby
his herb-garden gift.

God, I wish I
could be buried
in my vineyard,
so my blood seeps
downward in that
dark soil, makes it
even richer. But my
corpse will be devoured
(near the wall of
Jezre-el) by dogs.
There's no use
crying: my spilled blood
will be licked up by dogs.
He'll have it, then,
my life, my vineyard,
as the wicked woman
promised. And I know
she played most
foully for it.
Knowing that the
dogs will lick the
queen's blood
some day ought to make
me feel a little better.

But it's hard to see much
justice in it, even then.

Sometimes you must
just believe you've
done the right thing,
even when it all
turns ugly, and your
children
inherit only your
belief, your memory,
your dog-torn
and blood-spattered
name.

IMPROVISATIONS ON
"MELODIES" OF JAMES WRIGHT

I

She'll always be a girl,
not too much older or
less free, woven as she
always was: of pure gold
thread and gauzy silver
yarn. And after nightfall
I'll lie here awake, like
all her little boys,
wondering, wondering.
She'll always open both
tanned hands and butterflies
will fly out, and neither
girl nor butterfly will ever
quite be sold, or bought,
with coin, or pain.
She'll always point across
our dreams at tiny boxes,
delicate and full of dust,
but we won't know until we
run to where she's pointing,
open them, expecting (always)
butterflies, or tiny pools
of molten gold. And we'll lie here
awake again, her little boys,
wondering, wondering.

II

Maybe it will heal:
our fear of love.
When every man of
us is caught, and
every woman, when
we all confess not
what we did for love
but what we did in
fear of love. When
every woman of us,
every man, stands
penitent here by
our last sea. When
the princes of the
sea, and princesses,
cast off their robes
and walk, with naked
grace, on water to
our beach. Oh
maybe it will heal.

III

There haven't
been so many,
each loved in
some true way.
Why did they
touch me? Did
we not know
any other
language?
Could they
feel some
warm voice
singing from
my skin? They
owe me nothing.
I hope they
could feel me
singing.

MONEY, AND
LAST ADVICE

He plans to o.d.
on the substance,
wants to be dead.
He knows that, if
you need the stuff,
there'll always be
an old wreck (half
out, completely
down) who'll sell,
death penalty or
not. So he finds
him, pays his
poverty, advises
him to "buy food,
get yourself in
flesh." Then (in
the other city)
just before he takes
the poison, he gives
money to a buddy,
advises him to "live,
be prosperous."

Romeo & Juliet
Act V Scene I

449

SQUIRREL

Shirley's late for
work again. This time
she says, well, her
car hit a squirrel,
and she took the
poor thing to a vet.
Her boss, of course,
does not believe her:
this time Squirrely
Shirley's fired.
Years from now, that
grey-haired couple
will recall their
early breakfast being
interrupted by a
woman knocking at
their door, asking if
they had some kind of
box to put an
injured squirrel in.

PEACE ISLAND

You swim here
to Peace Island
when you can,
this place of
love and healing.
And you envy me
because I live
here all the
time. But you
must realize the
island changes
magically at
your approach.
With your first
footprint on the
beach, the sand
glows pink as if
reflecting roses.
The lonely wind-cries
turn to birdsongs.
And the island
hermit's ashen fire
re-kindles. It is
a place of love
and healing, this
Peace Island you
create each time
you swim here.

PARENTHESES

I drove (alone) this
afternoon, across
the bridge to Canada,
but what I wanted
wasn't there.
I walked (just me) four
blocks near where I
live, but ended up
where I began.
I listened (by myself)
to songs two people
should have danced to.

I sit here (solitary) as
the memories begin:

We drove (together) from
the front curb to the parking
lot, and found us there.
We walked (next to each other)
three blocks to a pub, and we
were waiting there for us.
We danced, and touched (in
harmony), and music played
inside us after it was done.

OVER, AFTER
ALL THESE YEARS

Suddenly over. Admit it,
and walk. I fight back
the image: her spreading
naked, him riding in her
body's groove.

Admit that it's over, and
walk. Sorrow turns angry,
repeats childish sing-songy
words: "the powder to blow
her to hell!" "She's not
worth the powder to blow
her to hell!"

My letter still unmailed.
Bottom of the fourth long
painful page, I'd add:
"P.S., You are not worth
the powder…" But I don't.

Soft from somewhere, I
hear a song (her kind,
country), one I used to
hear a lot – a record I
bought when we met: "can
be worth the world." "She
can be worth the world
if somehow you can touch
her at all."

"touch her at all." And
I know my stylus has been
stuck in that groove
all these years.

SHOPPING WITH BILL: THE LAST TIME

People turn to look – the tiny
white-haired man limps slowly
along, pushing the huge shopping
cart; holds on to make walking
a bit less hard.

> And I want to say, "Hey, people, not
> many months ago, this man taught me in
> his bible class, and he was eloquent:
> "If God be for us, who can be against...?"

Bill can't see much, but oh he loves
to shop, buy things for others, oh
he hates to give it up! A woman blinks
as he comes this close to her cart. He
never bumps things, just needs to be
that close to know something is there.

> And I can hear him quoting (he didn't need
> to read it) "He that spared not his own son, but
> delivered him up for us all..."

Even this near he can't read the signs,
so I do. It's expensive. He remembers
when it cost a whole lot less. "That's
raisin bread, Bill. It's a dollar eighty-
nine." "Highway robbery," he says, "but
let's get it; she really likes it."

> "We are more than conquerors through him
> that loved us... Neither death, nor life,
> nor angels..."

At the checkout, he counts his money
slowly slowly. The cashier tries to be
nice but looks impatient. Customers

behind us grumble a little, but show
respect for Bill's age…and dignity.

> "nor principalities, nor powers, nor things
> present, nor things to come…"

We push the cart together to the parking
lot. I put the bags into the car. He's
very tired, can hardly walk, but wants to
push the cart back to the store, "to make
it easier for someone else."

> "nor height, nor depth, nor any other
> creature, shall be able to separate us
> from the love of God."

QUARANTINE AT THE
NURSING HOME

I'm unwelcome here today.
I can't hang my coat near
the entrance, sign my name
as visitor, my mother's
name as resident, "son"
as relationship. I can't
walk down the corridor
that smells of urine-bloated
catheters, past open doors
where musty silent white-
haired women stare ahead
at nothing, or at death.
I'm no more welcome here
today than death. The
quarantine's to keep us
both out. I'd like to
see my mother, how her
cough is. But maybe all the
pale frail ladies have a
cough today. And if I went
inside, looked straight
into some pairs of staring
eyes, I'd find myself less
welcome there than death.

APOLOGY

Looking out the
window through
the rain: like
trying to see
what I was feeling
when we talked
last night. I'm
sorry. I never
want our talks
to be like that.
I really am, and
work at being,
positive and
pleasant almost
all the time.
I guess I just
think if we were
together more,
we would make
each other really
happy, not just
keep each other
from being sad.

VARIATIONS ON AN ANSWER
FROM ROBYN

for Karen

I asked her once
(she could be oh
so wise about us
all but Robyn) what
about friends making
love? "It's not,"
she said, "a good
idea." Maybe – this
is me now – maybe
the problem's words:
love is abused to
mean too many things.
We don't sort out –
we slap the L word on
two hundred different
feelings. Maybe we
(you, I) just love
each other much too
well to ever say it
with those clumsy
lovely things called
bodies. Could we – I
admit that it's a
scary thought – but
could we have a more
important kind of love?

TURNABOUT

I guess my turnabout
seems to make no more
sense than some of his.
And we both know he's
crazy. If there's a
difference (I think
there's a big one)
it's in the motivation.
I thought you'd agree
that I should leave,
agree with all the
books that say to be
alone, be independent,
deal with self and
situation. God knows
I don't want to leave –
you are the only place
I want to be. But it
seemed right then, as
right as anything these
crazy heat-wave days.
I told you. And your
reaction bowled me over.
After "devastated,"
your voice caught, tears
started. I spent time
with people, but my heart
and my distracted mind
were there with you.
And when I got home
late last night, I left
you messages, my turn-
about. All they're saying
I've said many times
before: Just *show* me
that you *care* about me:
I'll be here for you.

Fourteen Translations

ALWAYS THERE

I need to not look at myself anymore
              and to forget
To talk with people I don't know
To cry out and not be heard
For nothing all alone
I know everyone and each of your steps
I want to tell and have no one listen
Heads and eyes turn away from me
Toward night
My head is a full heavy ball
Which rolls across earth with little sound

Distant
Nothing behind me nothing in front
In the empty space I descend to
Gusts of wind
Blow around me
Cruel and cold

They come from doors not completely closed
On memories still not forgotten
The world like a clock stops
The people are suspended for eternity
An aviator descends on a thread like a spider
Everyone dances lightly
Between sky and earth
But a ray of light has come
From the lamp you forgot to turn off
On the landing
Ah it's not finished
Forgetting is not over yet
And I still need to learn to know myself.

- Translated from the French of Pierre Reverdy

AFTER MALRAUX'S *LAZARE*

Why

conscious of having "lost touch"

during this walk along the top

of my wall above against the sea

Why

stupefied by being "cut off from

the earth" conscious of no longer

"knowing where I am"

Why

at this strange poignant moment

do I wonder whether man was born

the first time that he murmured

at his first sight of his first corpse

Why

BETRAY

My fingers dip in
tears, your eyelids
clothe bare truth.
Your touch hurts me
by not including love.
Lonely, silent, scared
in shadows, we press
truth upon each other's
cheeks, then rush to
wash it off. In vein
our blood declares
we betray truth.

- Suggested by Sigurdur
Magnússon's poem "betrayal"

462

MY LOVE

She stands on my
eyelids, her hair
in my hair. She's
the color of my
eyes, the shape
of my hand. My
shadow surrounds
her, like sky
around a rock.
She never closes
her eyes, never
lets me sleep.
Her daydreams make
bright sunlight
disappear, make me
laugh, cry and
laugh, make me
speak when I've
nothing to say.

(after Paul Éluard)

THE IRON BRIDGE

I'm sure that there is, even now,
at the far end of that long street
I walked down as a child, a pool
of oil, a spread of sticky death
       beneath that black sky.

In the years since, poetry has
separated its waters from the
other waters. Beauty and color
can't hold it: it longs for
       iron and for night.

It sustains a long yearn of
dead river bank. An iron bridge,
leaping into even darker night
toward the far bank, becomes its
       only memory, its only love.

(Free translation from the
French of Yves Bonnefoy)

THE SCREECH-OWL

The night is a vast sleeping city,
and the wind blows. It has come from far
to our bed's shelter, this midnight
in June. You sleep, I'm beckoned out to
windy coasts where hazelnut trees tremble.
A cry comes, quavers near, flits away,
a gleam escaping through the woods, a
shade wheeling about in its hell.
(This cry in the summer night, how much
I could say of it, and of your open eyes.)
It's only a screech-owl, crying from
deep in these suburban woods. Already
our bodies smell of the decay of daybreak,
already beneath our warm skin the bones prick,
and stars fade at the corner of our street.

(Free translation from
Philippe Jaccottet)

LEAVETAKING

The horizon leans

      The days become longer

      Journey

A heart leaps in a cage

      A bird sings

      It is going to die

Another door is about to open

      At the end of the corridor

      Are shining

      A star

A dark woman

      The lantern of the train which is leaving

- Translated from the French
of Pierre Reverdy

WINTER, 1947

Daytimes in school, that somber swarming fortress.
Early evenings I'd walk home beneath the signs.
Then, whispers from no lips, "Wake up, sleepwalker!"
And everything would point up to The Room.

The fifth floor, above the back yard. The lamp
Burned in a circle of terror every night.
I'd sit on the bed, without eyelids, watching
Re-run movies of the thoughts of the mentally disturbed.

As if that were necessary…
As if the last of my childhood had to be
Broken into pieces to pass between the bars.
As if that were necessary…

I'd read in books of glass but I'd see only
The stains that worked their way through the wallpaper,
The stains that were the living dead
Who wanted to have their portrait painted.

Till dawn, when garbage men would come
And rattle garbage cans down in the yard.
Like ringing grayish peaceful bells,
They'd lull me into morning sleep.

(Free translation of
Tomas Tranströmer's
"Från Vinter, 1947")

IMAGES

Today if I listen to the

       sound of the days

what will I hear

only days dropping

into the deep unknown?

One is built of reflections,

one has no more body

than a knot of water and

       reflected light.

Life gradually turned

       into images,

distilled to images

       filtered inside us.

A poet transmits the purest ones.

A body of images, of memory.

       (After Philippe Jaccottet)

THE COUPLE

They turn out the light, its white bulb glows
a second, then dissolves, like a tablet
in a glass of darkness. Then, lift-off:
the hotel walls shoot up to midnight heaven.

Love movements become gentle, and they sleep,
but their most secret thoughts begin to blend
the way two colors, meeting, run together
on the dampened paper of a schoolboy's painting.

It is silent, dark. But the town edges near
tonight. With window lights out. Houses have come.
They stand crowded, waiting, very near,
a mass of people, no expression on their faces.

(Free translation from
Tomas Tranströmer's
"Paret")

469

THE ROADS OF FATE

The roads of fate: I measure them with my own life
And think about them, half without thought.
Days when the green grain billowed,
When the cuckoo cried, counting the things that last
And peasants followed the plows under the wind –
With silent understanding, I fused these.

I gladly bend beneath the weight of thorns and dead wood,
The air's a crystal tambourine your fingers gently shake,
I am attended by the slender poplars.

Your goodness is like old sunlight on branches about to bud.
I am with you in silence.
White doves fly to your heart.

(After Heinz Piontek)

BELL SOUND

Everything is snuffed out

The wind goes past singing

And the trees shiver

The animals are dead

There is no one left

Look

The stars have stopped shining

The earth no longer turns

One head is bowed

Its hair sweeping away the night

The last bell-tower left standing

Tolls midnight.

- Translated from the French
of Pierre Reverdy

PATIENCE

In the playing cards downcast beneath the lamp

like dusty collapsed butterflies,

across the tablecloth and the smoke,

I see what it is better not to see flush

when the ringing of the hour in the glasses

announces a new insomnia, the growing

fear to be afraid of the lessening of time,

the wearing-out of the body, the fading
                                      away of defenders.

The old man discards past images

and, not without repressing a tremor, watches

the icy rain push against the garden door.

(after Philippe Jaccottet)

SUN

Someone has gone away

In the room

There remains a sigh

The deserted life

The street

And the open window

A ray of sun

On the green lawn

- Translated from the French
of Pierre Reverdy

PINK CANDLE

There is one tall,
one beautiful pink
candle in the center
of the table of my
life, sometimes
burning steadily
with soft dependable
light; sometimes
flaming up the
twilight to a new
excitement; sometimes
waiting to be lighted,
peaceful in the
pleasant lull before
the glorious storm;
sometimes strong,
certain of lasting;
sometimes fragile,
flickering, nearly
out. I have tried
always to breathe
softly near the flame,
to light the candle
lovingly, to do what-
ever I can do to keep
the beautiful pink
candle in the center
of my life.

LONGING

This is not
frustration,
exactly.
We would
have to have
proximity
for that.
It isn't even
sadness,
quite.
The memories
are good,
the thoughts
are warm.
I don't know
what to call
this except
loneliness,
a very private
longing
for the person
I want to
be with.

THINKING ABOUT METAPHOR

for William Bronk

This "world" – there's no
unique intrinsic structure
we can grasp. But it's not
chaos. Laugh with the student
who says, "Gee, how could
astronomers find out the true
names of constellations way
out there!" And laugh with
the Walrus lumping ships with
shoes and kings with cabbages.
Not "is it true?" these days
but "is it useful?" The
question "what's the true
shape of reality?" is like the
same thing asked about a lump
of clay. Its shape's whatever
it's shaped into. The poet's
function: keep recreating
metaphor – not to be taken
word for word, but not to be
underestimated, either,
let alone lost sight of.

MONK AND NICA *

for Tommy Flanagan

Nica was there listening.
Whether he said 'I mean
you' or 'well you needn't'
Nica listened hard and
learned and damn near
understood the man that
maybe no one did. The
talkers shut up shop, the
praisers, pushers, went
to sleep it off together.
Nica was there listen-a-ning.
Oh Monk could stimulate,
exasperate. She took him
straight, no chaser, saw he
understood the world much
better than the world did
him, saw he could laugh.

She paid her dues, and paid
the rent on not-so-brilliant
corner flats criss-cross
off minor boulevards. He
wrote the gentle twilight

piece for his wife Nellie –

crepuscule. Nica's hour

began 'round minuit. She

heard his music limp

like a bird with a

broken wing, heard it

dance like Monk around

his chair, heard him

let the silence in,

surround the song with

emptiness. It was Monk's

dream, Monk's magic.

Nica was there listening.

* They had two of the most unlikely
names of modern times: Thelonious
Sphere Monk and the Baroness Pannonica
de Koenigswarter-Rothschild. As Tommy
says, "The relationship…was unique."

THE KITE POEM

The sky is so…
well, it's so VAST
and sometimes it
gets just plain
SCARY up there all
alone (when I'm the
kite), and GEE, it's
good to feel your
caring hand there at
the other end of that
long LONG string…
Hey, don't forget
that when it's your
turn to be flying,
I want you to be able
to feel just as SURE
of my hand keeping
you safely aloft…

LAST NIGHT

This place is empty now
in many ways: I'm here
alone, and almost every-
thing's been moved. This
morning I took down the
drapes (the drapes we
closed last night so we
could be alone together)
and carted them off to
my new place. I feel a
little too exposed, too
vulnerable here now, like
being in a fishbowl. Last
night we closed the drapes,
and opened ourselves
lovingly just to each
other. Last night we turned
out lights, and turned each
other on.
Although it was the first
time, and a little awkward,
some-
where in the midst of it, we
both felt love ease
quietly into the bed. This
place is empty now in many
ways. Last night it filled
and filled and overflowed
with you and me.

BEYOND

I think I know
the things our
bodies do; they're
lovely things,
remembered, praised.
But it all goes so
far beyond just
doing, and just
bodies. We can't
pin-point the
moment when the
magic starts to
happen. One minute
I'm stroking your
breasts, the next
we're swirling into
space, thrilled out
of both our human
minds, whirling to-
gether (more than
together: some wild
warm cosmic fusion).
And then we're back
acting like people
again (our gently
breathless interlude)
before we fly off
into – where do we
go, anyway!

LIKE THE OTHER LOVERS

We didn't quite
light up the dark
last night. No
rockets flared, no
sudden roses bloomed.
The golden wings
for once weren't
beating, and we
never really left
the ground.

But it was lovely
in the silent
darkness. Nerve
ends were soothed
and satisfied. There
was a sweetness in
our giving and our
trying.

We were like the
other lovers last
night, not swept up
in our own unique
transcendent sphere;
just loving quietly,
unselfishly, down
here on this
good earth.

HEAVEN

It starts with
our fingers on
each other's
skin and our
mouths kissing
all they can
reach There's
a thrilling
fulfilling full
joining of us
and we float
on a luster-
filled cushion
of passion Our
flesh swims like
fish in a
radiant pool We
rise like a
song into air
glowing golden
our windows all
open to magic
and musk We
throb like one
pulse We dissolve
in a lightburst
and Heaven is
jealous of us

URIRCHAR *

for Josh & Alice
Tsujimoto

Urirchar. A few pushed onto
boats before. A few pulled
later from the sea. The rest
are dead.

Urirchar. Only structures
left in sight – two cyclone
shelters. Otherwise flat mud
strewn with corpses, carcasses.

Urirchar. Winds a hundred miles
an hour. Tidal wave. A fifteen-
foot high wall of water. Last
thing thousands of the island
people ever saw.

Urirchar. Service man walks
down a line of people. Three
hundred still alive. Inoculates
them: typhoid, tetanus.

Urirchar.
             One needle, and one
prayer. The same needle, wiped
off after every jab.

Urirchar. "We can't change the
needle. Can't afford it. God,
give them resistance."

> * island 100 miles
> south of Dhaka,
> Bangladesh

THE POINT WILL BE REACHED

Highway (Youngmann, Oldman),
no red lights, no stop signs, no
turns. Spaces thru the median
like U-turns (drive back the
way he came?) but signs with
even that alternative X-ed out.
Driving a hearse, big shiny
spacious black and gleam. Inside,
deserted bar, sign turned off,
half-empty glasses, spilled stale
beer. A hearse. Slows down, pulls
over, stops, gets out. And walks.
He'll get there. The point will
be reached.

WAITING FOR YOU

I wait. The human wolves
have killed another Gandhi.
But a baboon's heart kept
Baby Fae alive a little
while. An hour ago I read
Paul Blackburn:

> Flesh come home, I
> seed you, it
> flies like a gull
> soars like a sound

- nearly the last entry
in his last journal. Words
for his wife, for all of
us, as his life ended. The
burn, the black spread,
of cancer. Can Paul have
been dead nearly fourteen
years? The elder Gandhi
more than thirty-five?

> Flesh come home, I
> seed you, it

flies like a gull

soars like a sound

I wrote, moments ago, a
note to Don, a friend whose
heart has been attacked
again. After you leave, two
or three hours from now (but
you're not even here yet),
I'll write to Dave, whose
accident tore holes in his
memory.

I try to tear from my memory
the wolves, and even the
baboon. I wait for you, need
you to fly with me, to soar
together like one gull.
Weighed down with heavy
thoughts, it seems we ought
to let the flesh come home.

MICHELLE IN
THE POOL

The sunlit water
sparkles blue this
happy-second-birthday
-plus-one-day. Her
feet, her chubby
legs, decide the
water's warm. Her
white suit's red
stars blue stripes
spangle with her
every kick and splash.
Michelle's delighted
when the water silvers
high, ecstatic when
her mommy catches her
bold leaps: one, two,
 THREEEEE!
A little timid jumping
out to someone else,
but Mommy: one, two,
 THREEEEEE!
She grabs a quick
breath, then, "Again!"

We do it many times
again again. Michelle's
enchanted by a tiny
swimming frog: her eyes
widen, sparkle blue as
water. Grandpa helps
Froggy up and out of
his big puddle, and
Michelle watches as
he hops away. "Again!"
But this time there's
no instant encore.
Froggy's all gone, and
we have to be content
with sunlight, sparkle,
silver, leap and splash
again   again   again

OPPOSITES BLEND

blue music

orange tiger

lilies hot

sunshine cool

breeze your

lips my ear

pale sheets

tanned bodies

feminine male

opposites blend

into one

believable

    incredible

afternoon fore

   -noon

TRANSFORMED

Although I'm here and
driving empty street-
lamped blocks, we're
still there lying
together in the dark-
ness we've transformed,
eyes bright as birds
(looking at everything,
not quite seeing any-
thing), hands feeling,
feeling carefully,
more gently than we
ever thought they could.

Although you're now
re-climbing empty
ceiling-lighted stairs,
we're still there lying
together in the magic
darkness, flesh
eloquent and awed,
bodies pronouncing new-
discovered words like
"thrill," like "heaven,"
bodies transformed
                into one.

THE YEARS AND THE
WORD AND TONIGHT

We didn't need to
spend a lot of time
remembering. The
years had not left
that kind of gap.

We talked, of course,
and that was good.
We didn't say the
word, but it was
there, drawing us
close. The word soon
to be flesh. The
word inevitable.

Tonight darkness
merges, blends into
light; receiving
becomes giving. A
sleepy little boy's
head on your shoulder
in the light becomes
my head here on your
breast in darkness.

In the night our
hearts instruct us;
bodies dwell secure.
Our warmth is wound
around inside each
other. Years have
left no gap.

PROSE POEM

Why is it that I'm always a little nervous when I'm going to see you, like a kid going to meet his date. I worry about my hair having blown around in the wind all afternoon at Allentown, about my unpolished boots looking even crumbier than usual. When I do arrive why does something happen to make me more awkward. Like the presence of your mother, especially knowing she doesn't want to be seen. Why, when it seems natural and right for us to touch, to kiss, do we seem almost to avoid it. After I'm with you a very few minutes why does it seem we've never been apart. Like we've been married ten years and our offspring is roller-skating down the driveway, grabbing the backs of our chairs. We're drinking instant coffee and not knowing the answers to trivia questions and ending up with silly "words" like FAKMGKE and like FUNA. You're erasing your suede skirt. I'm eating your apple-cake. You're waving "not goodbye." I'm driving off. That night you're calling me for a ride to the airport. Why is it I wake up the next morning from a vivid dream of touching and kissing (right and natural), of erasing all our clothes and being married in a total warm remembering how wonderful my fakmgke and your funa felt and how we loved the instant way we knew the answers as we came together. And then realize there are ten hours before I even pick you up to drive you to your plane to wave my "not goodbye."

FOR JOSH AND ALICE,
BACK FROM BANGLADESH

 The children love;
the people will believe.
The kite of faith sails
along the eastern sky.

"To see ourselves
as others see us."
Josh, Alice, thinner, but
somehow not older, smile.
(And we say, "Welcome,
welcome home!")

Faces, eloquent in silence,
all human, not all happy –
baby, child, woman, man –
eyes haunted, haunting
in their search. To see
others as we see ourselves.
To retain their eyes
in memory, in mind,
when they are out of sight.

The children run along
and watch the kite.
The children love;
the people will believe.

POEM ABOUT YOU

The room is dark,
a little chilly,
but you slip into
beneath-the-blankets
sleep, begin to fill
with lovely thrills
of warmth, such soft
sensations, to be
kissed and stroked,
to walk on air, to
climb a twilight
hill, lie curled
atop it, cuddled,
fondled gently, the
stimulation altering
in urgency, changing
like music, adagio,
andante, allegro,
to begin to dance
on air, accommodate
each movement to each
change in rhythm,
sigh as tempo drives
and escalates to reach
exquisite tension, the
flowers on the hill
explode, the petals
float out everywhere,
you wake in mid-
explosion, feeling
love and love
and love.

SALVADOR

late at night, after
writing to Carolyn Forché

No music

no words either

bodies

lie there lined up

lie there

tears already dry

dead men sing from

holes once mouths this

frigid night

a corpse sweats blood

no music words

no body either:

"disappeared"

dried up like tears

MOVING

I've been moving
books again. I
have so many.
And I want each
in its place. Not
many people have
bookshelves along
their bed: I have
five hundred books
of poetry. Do they
bother you? They
could be over-
whelming. So many
words so close
beside the bed –
your side, the
times you're here.
But I guess nothing
bothers either of
us when we're together
here, each in our
place. We concentrate
on us. And sometimes
we're so moving, over-
whelming, we make a
poetry that all the
books on all the
shelves could never
translate into words.

RAIN FALLING

Dark of course and rain keeps falling,
seeping into earth where much is buried
that we love, so many that we love;
making love has seemed akin to rain, a
joining humanly as rain does earthily,
a raining from person deep into person,
causing flowers to spring into a world
that would not have and needs them, rain
in darkness, and what is who is buried
lies in darkness, warm we hope but possibly
not dry, washed by rain, washed, and rising
from earth a mist across earth's face above
the faces we almost remember, mist returning
to its source to be made into rain, to fall
of course keep falling, seeping into earth
where many are, much is.

QUIET AFTER THE GLORY

I think we lay down on
a hill above a town, where
tiny lights winked off or
on in darkness far below.
Or did we lie down in a
valley, and the tiny lights
were stars, and they were
far above us? Or were we
the lights, our well-used
bodies lighting up the
early-morning dark? Anyway,
we got up, quiet after the
glory, and traveled silently
through empty streets to
sleep in separated beds. And
when we each woke up, we found
snow fallen on the hill and
town and valley. All the lights
and stars had gathered, had
spread themselves like blankets
soft across the well-used
body of the earth.

THOSE WORDS

You have been
writing notes
to me again

It has been
good to see
your words

The lack of
words can be
a white space
or an enclosing
silence

I love you
very much

See how those
words fill their
portion of this
white page

We speak them
and the silence
goes away

RUNNING THROUGH THE PARK, SIGNING

for Karen

Running this fresh morning
through the park near the
river you feel happy. You
sign "happy": bring the
flat palm, fingers pointing
left, outward and upward
on your chest. You're in
an "up" mood. You practice
handshapes, finger-spelling,
as you run, surprised that
so few people stop to stare.

Your eyes have changed:
people look different,
gestures, this poem printed
on this page, worn steps,
weathered sculptures, all
look new. Around you
mundane has turned magical.
You needed a new language
and you fell in love
              with one.

At corners, you see people
signing, waiting for traffic
lights to change. To learn
you eavesdrop, even join
their silent conversations.
"Sign": move both extended
index fingers pointing up,
palms facing, in alternating
circles out around each other
in front of your chest.

Because you hear, and others
don't, there is no sound you
take for granted now. At times
you wish you could be deaf.
You sign quite well, but don't
grasp all you see. Look is
listen, but it's more than
                          look.

"What is it like to 'hear' a
hand?" Hear fingers dance?
Your teachers are wonderful,
but so fast that you need to
bypass eyes and fingers,
center yourself in your solar
plexus. You're a hearing child
the deaf take slowly step by
step and guide into their world.

But this fresh morning you can
run in the park by the river,
form handshapes, finger-spell,
sign, and run, and sign.

CLOSE TO ANSWERS

Metallic clicks, snaps, whirs
are gone. So is the music.
The stylus drops in a silent
groove, the record turns,
plays without a sound. Outside
clear muted drops fall in
hushed grass. I come close to
answers. Silence thinks as I
do, fits itself to my thoughts.
I can almost (almost) penetrate,
surround myself with silence,
be filled with it. Silence
sings truth. I almost hear it.
Pale flickers, pale flashes
cut across the dark sky with
no sound. I blink, think: One
moment of illumination – could
it be a sign? I feel that close.
The record ends, the stylus
rises from the groove, returns
to its metallic perch amid
whirs, snaps, one final click.
I hear God's rain fall
out there in the dark.

ORANGE AND YELLOW

Mark Rothko, 1903, born in Dvinsk,
Russia. Prominent American painter,
Abstract Expressionist. "All of art
is the portrait of an idea." Committed
suicide in New York City, 1970. In
Buffalo, in 1970, I started working
at the Suicide Prevention Center. But
Mark was in another city, and he didn't
call. In 1982, at Albright-Knox, I'm
looking at his painting "Orange and
Yellow" (1956), 91 by 71 inches.

I stand close, look

close, Mark, enter your

orange environment,

feel the texture of

your yellow town

surround me. Intensely

intimate: nothing between

me and your tragedy,

nothing between this

earlier work and the

late you. Your painting

- or your ghost – haunts

me. (Yeats said a

ghost was someone who

felt strong emotion

just before he died,

strong enough to

hold his molecules
together after death,
perhaps for years.)
I'm pulled apart,
then gradually calmed.
Mark, in this work,
your anguish has
become serene. Light
everywhere, pure yellow
light, pure orange.
Before you, behind, are
darker paintings, darker
years. But right now
you're with me inside
this portrait of a
great idea, this
luminous suspension,
this floating wall,
painted with wingtips
dipped in angel orange,
dipped in Rothko yellow.

RUSH TO MIDSUMMER

Carnations on the
bedside table –
one green, one
red – weren't
there to signal
"go" or "stop,"
so we rushed
lovelong out of
early March into
midsummer fields
where daisy petals
shone in sunshine
near a lake, and
what was even
better than the
rush was that
the world tipped
upside up and
inside in, and
left us catching
breath together in
each other's mouth.

BETWEEN, NOT READY

The time between, you know?
The time when you're not
ready? When four themes are
cross-creasing your
excedrined head – the new
phone book you never got
so half the numbers have
been changed; the birthday
game the stores are out of
but you need tomorrow so
you call; the hope to see
your woman for an hour: it's
been a week; the tape that
must be made this weekend
for your Tuesday play; and
then your friend is at the
door, you half-greet, half-
push-out, and feel like shit
because he even tries to help
and the look his face has
says you're one more phony
in a world full and you're
treating him the way the other
phonies do. The time when
you're not ready. The time,
you know, between.

TO...

To watch your car

sink into quicksand

in a junkyard: to

realize it twilight

when you thought it

dawn: to take a chance

and win, and not know

what to do with winning:

to touch a face as gently

as you can, because you

love it so much it might

turn into your own.

LAMPLIGHTING

Snowfall so white

it's silver.

Darkness among

the flakes. The

streetlamp lighter

thrusts his long

pole up into the

nearest lamp, which

soon begins to glow

with golden light.

He comes in snowy

silence, comes on

down the fallen

street, reaching

up into each dark

lamp, touching it

to light, to light,

to light.

LATE READING

remembering John Logan

A window right behind
his balding head; out-
side rain starting as
he read poems not of
sun or rain; late words
that smiled past (or
through) pain: words
transfused with honest
living, poems that slowly
drained him, part of his
heart giving. He read
that evening till his
voice cracked; turned to
pick up the books he'd
stacked behind him;
looked up at the window,
saw the rain descending;
turned back to us, laughed:
"Kind of a soggy ending…"

UP THERE ALONE

(in memory of David Fendrick's
one-man acting performances)

He made us

forget he was

up there alone:

the stage seemed

to fill with,

spill with humanity.

He talked to us

sometimes, us in the

audience, one at a time,

but mostly he talked

to the people on the stage.

They weren't there till he

talked to them,

but then they were.

The actor with the

velour voice, the man who

put the "Open All

Night" sign on the door

of the Club Soliloquy.

BLOWN UP

Fear is on the slide
under the microscope,
your fear of losing
him. Words are too big
to force out through
your lips, words like
"us," like "future."
His thin face, pillow-
color on the pillow,
has grown larger than
life is: a photograph
blown up, blown up!
He has become a planet,
huge and still, and you
a satellite revolving.
You want (and do not
want) to stop it: shrink
the swollen words and
face; prepare another
slide to replace fear.

POEM FOR PHIL

I

Listen. That bassoonist
is getting colors from
his instrument that
no one ever knew it
had. You do that, pour
colors from inside,
astonish people with
your rainbows.

II

When a lot of
people love you
and they know
you're dying,
all that love
raining softly
down on you
while you're
alive, flooding
you, setting you
adrift, float on
it, float quietly on
people's love a while.

SMALL QUESTIONS

Tell me, are the
windshield wipers more
important than the
glass? Everywhere, not
just on my car radio,
why do I understand
the music, lately,
better than the
words? Wet gray
mornings, why wake
earlier than bright ones,
wake, and drive the
streets like this?
Why not stay home,
and watch the TV
colors blur, or blot?

The radio: ironically,
the Grateful Dead are
still around, as much
as Prince, or Sting.
The Princes, one of
Denmark, one of Peace,
already asked the
biggest questions. Mine
are small. But, are
there other ways to
measure worth, besides
survival? And, does
caring deeply always
lead to sorrow? I mean,
are the windshield
wipers more important
than the rain?

SUGAR ROAD

Between Pine Ridge and
Eggert is a lonely road
named Sugar. It seems a
strange name for a road.
I drive it only as a
shortcut home. I'm not
a cemetery person, and
Sugar is a narrow road
between expanses of gray
cemetery. Metal fences
line the road on both
sides, and beyond them,
multitudes of graves.

If you drive on past
Eggert, Sugar turns to
Langfield, and people
are alive. If you turn
back and drive the other
way on Sugar, you'll
only reach more sections,
more expanses, of stone
cemetery. If you enter
the right gray stone
gate, and make the
proper turns, you'll
find me sometimes
(although I'm not a
cemetery person)
looking down on my
friend's stone. Last
time, I had to brush
snow off to read her
name and her brief
years. Last time, the
ground was so rock

hard I couldn't free
an urn her mother
wanted from the frozen
earth. My friend's
last years were lived
in California. But
she'd come back here
in the winter – "I
still need to see the
snow," she told me once.

If you are driving north
on Bailey, where the
street names sound like
law firms, or like under-
takers: Easton, Weston,
Erskine, Langfield, you
turn east on Langfield,
still driving past the
living people for a
while, and then when
you pass Eggert, you're
not on Langfield any-
more. And if, for once,
the sun is shining on
the snow, you understand
why they might name a
road here Sugar.

THE CORNER
OF MEMORIES

Walking fast, past
the wall, past the
shadow. Taking off
shoes at the white
sunlight's edge.
Walking fast, one
bare foot on cement,
one on grass.

Arriving, one
moment late, at
the corner of
memories. Watching
them drift off in
silence. Like grey
balloons, smaller
and smaller.

TWO RELATIONSHIPS

for Karen

I. Mourning Already

Lately she feels him
starting to withdraw.
(When they talked he said
he pushed her away
more as he felt more.
She has not seen him
often – does that mean
he's caring a lot these
days? should she be
flattered?) When he's
finished with her, she
expects to have to live through
a long period of
mourning. Since he won't
let her forget he plans
to abandon her one day,
she is mourning already.
She will most likely
stay with him as long
as she can bear it, or
as long as he'll allow it.

II. It's Just There

She doesn't want to
lose their friendship
or the potential
for it to be something
else. His love letters
are the only ones she's
ever had. What she
wants from him, how
close she feels it's
safe to get to him, she
can't say. But can't
imagine her life without
him. She's loved him so
long it isn't even some-
thing to be known: it's
just there. Her
thinking of him
never stops.

CHOICES

for Genie

Solitude, not loneliness

peace amid, not freedom from

fields of wildflowers, not flowerbeds

loved, not used

songs, not symphonies

special, not commonplace

solitude, not loneliness

peace amid, not freedom from

look out from, not look in at

content, not weary

involving, not isolating

anticipate, not fear

solitude, not loneliness

peace amid, not freedom from

WHICH END OF THE PHONE

Whether you're here
lying in my arms
or, like now, I'm
sitting late alone,
I always seem to
need you more than
sleep. Right now
I need to talk with
you. We had a good
talk, really two
good talks today.
But having doesn't
always do away with
need. I know that I
should sleep. I
have to get up
early, counsel people,
help them make it
through the morning.

But tonight I'd talk
to you for hours,
if that could be.
We'd talk of ending
dreams, beginning
knowledge, a garden
prophesied to be a
wilderness. And for
a while it wouldn't
matter which end of
the phone I'm on.
Writing to you helps
a little, this
little writing I've
just done. Goodnight,

love. I think I can
sleep now. Don't go
thinking that means I
don't need you more.

NOCTURNE

This is not the shore
of sound where every
special silence starts.
This is not the wood
of words where space
between is infinitely
precious. This is not
the hill of singing
where only mutes are
heard. This is the
night of lonely peace
that rises smokelike
from the love bed of
a brilliant afternoon.
This is the continent
the evening overhangs
with sky, and lights
the same stars over
Cambridge and New Orleans.

HENCE

"It's just the

same old body,"

you said, implying

I'd get bored

with what I

touch beneath your

clothes. Hey, love,

I'm bored like

Caesar (surrounded

by assassins), yell-

ing, "Hence! Wilt

thou lift up

    Olympus!"

DIALOGUE

Are we friends?
>The people who can't
>know we're lovers
>think we're friends.

Are we?
>To be friends with
>the one you love: a
>rare achievement.

I know it seldom
happens. But with
us I think it has.
>Have we given us a
>chance to know?

Enough chance that
I think I know.
>And I know, too. I
>just like hearing it
>from you.

It's so important,
isn't it?
>It's – Next to love,
>friendship is life's
>great offering.

Combined with love,
friendship becomes
…sublime.
>So now…we have it
>all?

We don't have
marriage. But, yes,
all the rest.
>"What all the others
>crave and seek for."

I – I love you,
friend.
>You are my friend,
>my love.

RIVER

I am part of

you are part

of we become

immersed in

touch and

movement are

one flow one

current passing

through and

through our

self is flowing

in one thrilling

river into this

calm water in

this afternoon

of peace is

part of you

are part of me

SUPPRESSED OVERTONES

For Karen

"The word pink has many overtones
one should suppress, especially
the erotic ones.

Because we are facing the purest."

- Philippe Jaccottet

A pink sky,

smoky dusty

pink:

the color

suffusing clouds,

smoke rising from

a fire somewhere,

dust settling.

You mentioned

in my poetry

through years

a single voice,

dependable you

called it, constant.

I have listened to so much

flute music lately – the

instrument the only simil-
arity – different artist,
different composition,
background, style. But the
flute dependable,
suffusing other elements,
rising through them,
settling, constant.

Pink dust
smothering
this fire,
pink smoke rising,
suffusing
these clouds.

PASS THROUGH

for James Wright
1927-1980

Raindrops. Follow

them deep into the

river. The river

would be cleaner

if I could have

my way and warmer

but it will be

cold and filthy so

what else is new

except you and the

raindrops? Follow

them deep past

blameless beauty

and past blame

past the muse that

could not swim

back up to you

past the demons and

divinities of change

down to where your

human lungs would

burst if you were
still what I still
think of as alive.
Pass like threading
an eye through the
small barely visible
small door. It looks
too small but you
will get through.
The swimming would
be easy if I could
have my way there
in the clear clean
ocean among the
rainwashed stars.

MISSING YOU

I thought, a little, I'd
indulge myself in missing
you. I'd play "miss you"
music like *Loneliness Re-*
turns or Larsson's andante
movement for piano, strings.
I'd read "miss you" poems
like Tranströmer's dream:
"her white body, the parts
left white by the bathing
suit." But that could drive
me crazy, knowing you're in
Florida, becoming tanned. I
think, a little, that I'd
better cool the "miss you"
stuff. Oh, yes, you're worth
it, love. I just don't know
if I can take it.

DRIVING

He's driving his car
slowly around her
block (around a-
round) past her
apartment (past it
past it) watching,
keeping an eye on,
what he thinks he
knows she's doing.
He's driving himself
crazy around her
block (around a-
round) past her
apartment (past it
past it) watching,
hoping to find out
what he doesn't
want to be true
because he's al-
ready decided
that it is.

AWAY

You have been away
more than we've been
together. I don't
understand your absences:
I never have. This time
it's Chicago, but the
city doesn't matter:
sometimes you've been
far away right here.
I love solitude, and
I get plenty of it:
I should thank you
for that, I suppose.
Loneliness is just a
state of mind, of
course. (See what
insights you have
helped me gain?) I can
enter into depths of
silence, or of music,
for that matter: enter
without worrying the
phone will ring, or
you'll come to the
door. I can concentrate
on what I'm doing; only
sometimes it seems all
I'm really doing is
enjoying solitude: like
loneliness, a state of mind.

FLAMES

Our early times together have
been lit and warmed by flames,
flames started with long fire-
place matches, or with matches
so short one of us would come
too close to getting burnt,

Flames in the fireplace flaring
suddenly from sheets of paper,
or building up more slowly from
tight rolls of newsprint, or
flames easing down to embers
from large chunks of wood we'd
carried in and placed inside
the fireplace carefully,

Flames that we fanned back into
being when they'd almost disap-
peared, a few flames that we
couldn't get back even when we fanned,

Flames rising gracefully from
yellow candles in the dining
room, as gracefully as music
rising from the stereo to fill
the house.

We were a little awkward about
some of it: singed finger, dusty
stylus, dark ash on the carpet,
but the mood was comfortable,
relaxed, the music was delightful,
the flames were part of something
growing, glowing,
in our early times
together.

MOURNING AFTER

To whom you left me, my love
may concern: I'll burn the
candle in its pot of gold at
both ends of the rainbow.
I'll roll out the drum and
bang the barrel slowly and
wish everyone good after-
morning and good noon. I'll
hold my fingers and I'll
cross my breath, shout
"Gloryosky Silver!" and
"Hi Yo Zero Away!" and end
up white as punch, pleased
as a sheet, and sign this
note to you, "Sincerely
hearted, Broken yours."

WORTHY

Judgment? I
thought I
knew a little
about love.
Now here's
Cid Corman
calling love
"the only
judgment man
is worthy of."
I'd never
thought of
love as judgment,
but now I do,
it seems the
highest kind, a
most amazing kind
for man to be
entrusted with.
I doubt his (and
my) worthiness.

CROCUS

Learn, yes, to live
like a crocus again:
burst through the
frozen spring turf.
No, not just watch
leaves become palely
green: no, not be
patient until earth
is warm: not wait for
blossoms, no, not
watch buds form.
Learn, yes, to break
right through rock
like a saxifrage.
Learn, yes, the pain
of the beauty of
being a crocus again.

WE NEVER WEREN'T

We never really
weren't, you know.
You loved me sadly
more grey noons than one.
The truths I told I told to you.
We touched much, many ways.
You stretched long ribboned
in my closed desk drawer.
I coiled and shone in your
shut jewel case. Does anyone
know anyone the way we know?
We never really weren't.

THE PLACE BETWEEN

White horses. Grey

horses. Not a dream.

Not a sound. Like a

vast patient waiting

room. Like dark green

veins in new leaves.

A forever changing

field. Grey horses

in the rain. White

horses in the snow.

THEY KNEW EACH OTHER BETTER

They knew each other
better than to blurt
blunt words that hurt.
They'd not bow-hunt
each other, not
search the other out,
bow drawn, in some
dim woods-end where
they'd have to nurse
hurts, turn inward from
new hurt. They'd not even
murmur words to wound.
They'd talk of (not walk on)
memory's footprinted beach,
to teach each other of (not
touch or make touch)
those too-tangible sands.
Disturb earth's nervous
bubbles? Probe till
trouble surfaced? They
knew each other better.

OUR LAST POEM

I thought at least
that we'd go out with
fireworks, or a bonfire
("conflagration" is our
kind of word), not like
this, not even together,
just me alone,
standing in the rain,
watching its soft splash
in the dull grey ashes.
Well, no one will have to
worry that left-over
flames will torch the
forest. It's not even
all that hard to
walk away,
with nothing but wet ashes
there behind me.
But oh God, what do I
do when sunrise comes
and comes, to show me
how we used to be!
The ashy smoke drifts
sadly toward the stars,
maybe toward the one
that's named for you.
I don't feel much like
looking up, even to
see a star.

TOO MUCH

I guess I want
too much: I
should do
guilt trips
for my greed:
to brush one
snowflake
from your
forehead each
December: to
kick through
fallen leaves
with you once
each October:
to place one
small bouquet
of daisies on
your table each
July: to watch
the sun rise
with you one
morning of each
April: to lie
down in your
arms each
night for thirty
thousand years

MORNING, DAY BEFORE SURGERY

Summer's naked exit is almost

clothed by mid-September misting

up the roadside into me. These

flower-colors (not quite blue,

not quite beige) are subdued,

less warm. They feel good to

the naked eye. But breaths of

less warm air inside me stir

uneasily at this quick spattering

of leaves like bright red blood.

INSIDE HIS EYES

He was the late
night city and
the city knew
and fit itself
within his
             boundaries.
I remember
looking in his
eyes and seeing
lighted windows
in tall dark
buildings, seeing
streetlights, neon-
lighted sidewalks,
even red green
yellow traffic
lights far back
inside his eyes.

WILD STRAWBERRIES

A narrow country dirt road.
I was pretty young. My father
stopped the car beside an
open field. The grass was
filled with small white
flowers, everywhere, white,
everywhere. "We'll come back
when they're berries. With
luck," my father said, "we'll
find them ripe, before the birds."

We came back, with baskets,
with my brothers. Dad had timed
it right. We could stoop anywhere,
and pick small red sweet berries,
anywhere. We boys stooped. Our
father picked, on knees, hands
quick as birds, then disappeared,
poked up his head in a far acre
of the field, still picking,
filled five baskets while we each
filled one. The knees of his grey
workpants, his hands, arms up to
elbows, all were juicy red. We
boys were caught red-handed,
happy guilt stains
              on our mouths and chins.

AGELESS

"When I grow too old to dream,
I'll have you to remember…"
        - Hammerstein-Romberg

I'm feeling ageless

today, one in a series

of sunshiny June mornings.

My mother, who was 87

the month before Mother's

Day, comes slowly to the

breakfast table, using

her walker. "The music is

pretty," she says. I must

have it on loud: she can't

hear well. We both look

out the kitchen windows

as we eat our cereal.

The white perennial roses

are blooming, the ones

my father planted long

before he died ten years

ago at 82. The music is

my oldest classical

record: I bought it over

thirty years ago, "That's

Segovia," I tell my mother,

"playing guitar. He died
yesterday. He was 94."
He's playing a passacagli
and corrente by Frescobaldi,
who'd be four hundred four
years old this year. And
I remember years and years
ago my mother's favorite
song was "When I grow too
old to dream." I wonder
if she dreams now. I wonder
how I'll feel if I should
grow too old to…well, to
hear soft music play; too
old to…remember. But
today I'm feeling ageless.

WHERE ANNA IS TONIGHT

Where Anna is tonight,
the leaves do not fall
from the trees, form
brown and sodden heaps;
one cannot foresee winter
in grey shapes of cloud.
Dull rain will never
wash away the sun
where Anna is tonight.

Where Anna is tonight,
no birds will fly off
southward in a storm
of wings; no people
burrow sadly deeper into
dark woods, into leaves.
No melting snow will drown
fires into greasy smoke
where Anna is tonight.

"DIRECTING" OPHELIA

What a role! One every actress thinks she
wants, and every woman sort of gets. Start
at the end of life. They'll bury you with
much-maimed rites in mad rogue Yorick's grave
and sing no requiem, remembering your death was
doubtful. Laertes' elegy will be a shout of pain: *Churlish*
priest, my sister will become an angel while you
howl in hell. Your funeral service will
include brother and lover brawling in
your grave about which one loved you more. Lie
very still through all the hubbub, not just
because you're dead but as sweet contrast.
The audience gets only this last vision to put
with Gertrude's image of your death: you with
fantastic garlands in the weeping brook, your
garments, heavy with their drink, pulling you
from melody to muddy death.

What a role! Forget to act.
But don't forget the woman that you are
inside the maid they all talk at, about,
and (rarely) to. Inside obedience, be free.
What is said at you is mostly nonsense:
let the audience do the listening.
Everyone will talk about you
when you're dead. The Queen
will even talk to you then: *I hoped*
you'd be my Hamlet's wife. I thought
to deck your bride-bed, not to strew
your grave.

Yours is not an antic disposition. You are
truly mad. It springs all from your
father's death. And they will let you die

because they know you're crazy.

Someone sits and watches you drown,
watches so closely he can give the
Queen every tiny detail. What patience
that observer has! How long he must
sit there! He could rescue you ten times
but it doesn't cross his mind. He's too intent
on accuracy of observation, and on taking
copious notes. Notes on the flowers in your
garland – crowflowers, nettles, daisies, and
those long purples you'd call dead man's fingers,
but shepherds give them grosser names. He should
save your life, not study horticulture. Notes
on how a branch broke and you fell in the brook,
on how your clothes spread wide and bore
you up. He has time to save you, but you're
crazy, see? Notes on you chanting snatches
of old tunes until your garments, heavy with
their drink, pulled you down from melody
to muddy death. And only then this patient keen
observer jumps up, and rushes to the Queen,
and says that crazy Ophelia has drowned. You're dead.

BURNED

They say she'd written
something in the basement
earlier, then burned it.
I think it was a poem.

She must have been able
to hear the winter
rain hit the windows,
run down like tears.

It was the wrong
time for rain: it
didn't help anything
grow or stay alive.

It fell into the
melting snow and
everything turned
dirty grey.

In the basement she
stroked her cat with
silent desperation,
wrote something,

burned it. Suddenly
her last split-second
was a weapon's roar.
People don't burn

suicide notes. I think
it was a poem.

HENRY WINTER DAVIS

His middle name was Winter.
His voice, in oratory, was silvery,
seductive, "clear and cold as starlight."
Wanted end, right now, to slavery:
no patience with gradual emancipation,
nor any Lincoln plan. Hated Lincoln,
aimed to pull down his administration,
let Congress control reconstruction,
subjugate that Southern foreign nation.

His middle name was Winter.
When Lincoln pocket-vetoed his
pet reconstruction bill, he stood
a full hour, "pale with wrath,"
waving his arms, denouncing
Lincoln to the starless summer sky.
But politics reverse opinions and
positions suddenly. Once Lincoln ran
for re-election, the wintry silver voice,

they said, would declare Lincoln patriot,
abolitionist, hope of nation and unity.
Not so. He kept repeating his chill
anti-Lincoln speech and lost his own
votes. Ousted Congressman, unwanted
orator, H. Winter Davis frostily made way
for those who hated Lincoln more.
One's middle name was Wilkes.

"LADY VELVET"?

In the beginning was
the voice. The voice
was hers. He hadn't
seen her yet, so all
he had to go on was
the voice.

"Velvet whispering
would say these
words," he thought.
"Satin speaking would
sound like this."

He began to see
colors: soft pastels,
mauves, indigos.
And a name came
to him: "Lady
Velvet." All that
just from her voice.

And then…he saw her.

BLUE WALK

The gentle big man rose,
lifted his sugar blue horn,
and blew. The blues songs
he chose walked me along

under blueleaf trees
in some lost dark park,
walked me in footprints worn
across a blue lawn long gone,

walked me so slow so breezy
in my old easy blues shoes.

THEY USED TO TELL

They used to tell, old gray-brown men,
how they could hear his trumpet clear
and loud across the widest stretch of
river; how, children, they'd stay up, not
go to bed like they were told, 'cause he'd
be playin' over at the hall. They all out-
lived him thirty, forty years, of course,
and now they're all gone, too. He had a
drummer with him, and a bass, they said,
and played tunes he made up along the
way. Nobody's left who heard him, or said
they did; he made no records, so we can't
prove he really played at all.

THE SHORE YOU REACH

I'd spread me
like a cloak
across the
      roily mudpond
a dark
grey morning,
and let you
      dance across,
but the soaked soil
      of the puddle's
      stark far shore
would probably
be lost in fog,
and bullfrog voices
bobbling from the pond
would croak
      cross warnings:
"Wade." "Don't
cloak-dance." "Wade."
Because the bobbling
bullfrogs know,
      and teach,
that soon or late
the fog lifts, and
the shore you reach
      by dancing
is surely not
the same shore
      you reach
when you wade.

THEY

One thought there'd be
pure absence – but no,
they're here, they fill.

It's that the darkness
(as if it were light)
shows through them.

If nothing opened, did
they rise like smoke from
depths of themselves?

One thought there'd be
sheer lack of sound – but
no, their silence whelms.

It's that, voiceless, they
pray their own elegy: not
quite heard, unforgotten.

THE LAND

for Carolyn Forché

The burned land had
grown thistles, grown
brown thorns. Something
frowned up from the
dust on flowers,
from the ash on
olive trees. Someone
tried, through nostrils
dried with blood, to
smell the sea. And suddenly
it was too late to turn
the rage of wind or
water, bid the coming
storm subside. The
cursed and thirsty
land would drink in,
drown in, all the
rain that fell.

PROMISE

In the spring of 1936, I was six years old. Playing hide-and-seek, I stepped off our bottom cellar stair in the dark, and nearly drowned. The melted snows and heavy rains had flooded our whole cellar. Cold filthy water came up to my shoulders (I was small for my age) and I half-panicked, but then I grabbed the railing and held on, and yelled.

The week of my sixth birthday, thousands of miles away, Osip Mandelstam, drowning in exile in cold filthy Veronezh, finished three poems. People say he didn't, couldn't, write them down, he spoke them out, screamed them in the air, rushing headlong on crooked streets. "They, not you nor I," Osip said, "they have total control over all the endings of words." I picture him holding on to a railing, and yelling that.

His wife wrote down the words of each finished poem. "Forgive me for what I say," Osip said (or screamed), "Quietly, quietly, read it to me." I have lived sixty-four years since my near-drowning. Osip died in 1938. Osip lived, altogether, only forty-seven years. For parts of them he was numb, unspeaking, glassy-eyed, from horrors in camps.

Life, as the saying goes, life has been good to me, more than expected, much more than promised. Shakespeare had Kent and Edgar ask "Is this the promised end? Or image of that horror?" At the end of the last poem he wrote, "What will be," Osip said, "what will be is only a promise."

Notes

NO SONGS BUT WHISPERS

THE FLOWERS: Suggested by the painting "Dandelions," by Ted Striewski.

POEM FOR BERT LAHR: Shortly before his death, Lahr expressed an interest in acting the role of King Lear. He had moved from pure comic roles such as the cowardly Lion in *The Wizard of Oz*; and a potato chip commercial, "you can't eat just one"; to such demanding roles as that of one of the tramps by the side of the road in *Waiting For Godot*.

WINDOW WINE: Based on a passage from *The Wisdom Of The Desert*, translated by Thomas Merton.

SUMMER STORM: Suggested in part by the print of that name by Robert Freeland.

SWEET RAIN: A reaction to the composition of that name by Stan Getz.

THE HOUR BEFORE THE WIND

DEEP: Suggested by the painting "The Deep," by Jackson Pollock.

AGON: Suggested by Lynn Chadwick's sculpture "Agon," at Buffalo's Albright-Knox Art Gallery.

FIRST BASEMAN: Dedicated to the memory of Mel Snyder, a polio victim who became a legendary baseball player in my home town, Lancaster, NY.

WARM BROOMS

DRAG TREES ALONG THE SNOW: Commemorates the last of the annual Christmas tree burnings in Delaware Park, Buffalo.

HELL IS MEASURED IN MEN: The music by Bill Evans is "Turn Out The Stars."

THREAD: The translation of Porchia is from W.S. Merwin's *Voices*, as is the one in I WANTED TO GIVE YOU.

FAUN: Owes debts to Debussy, Mallarme, and Nijinsky, among others.

IDA LUPINO: Based partly on the composition of that name by Carla Bley, recorded by Paul Bley.

THE POEM ABOUT HUMPHREY AND THE LEAVES: Refers to the visit by Hubert Humphrey to the U.S. Senate just before his death.

ALWAYS A LEGACY: Based on a wonderful letter from John Milner. I wish also to thank John for his advice and encouragement on all my books of poetry.

I WANT TO TALK ABOUT YOU: Suggested by the composition of that name, written and recorded by John Coltrane.

EN OTRA CALLE: The Spanish words are by Octavio Paz. Translated by Gregory Rabassa, they say "My steps along this street / Resound / Along another street / Where / Only the fog is real."

DEER PATH: Suggested partly by the composition of that name, composed by Glen Moore and recorded by Oregon.

FOR DANA, IN WICHITA: The French words and part of the situation were suggested by Dostoyevsky's *The Idiot*, in which Myshkin persuades the children of a town to cheer up an abused young woman by singing their love to her, "Nous t'aimons, Marie."

WILDFLOWERS

TRANE AS OMNEDARUTH: In San Francisco, at the time of John Coltrane's death, a church was formed by King Bishop Ha'qq XIX. It was devoted to, was founded for, and celebrated the music and spirit of Coltrane, called Omnedaruth, or Compassion.

GOMER TO HER HUSBAND, HOSEA: Hosea 1: 1-11

AS I MIGHT HOLD A BIRD

During the writing of these poems, I first found, and then listened very closely to the music of the Swedish composer Lars-Erik Larsson, especially his concertinos for viola, for horn and for flute.

EVENING EVERYTHING

SOLILOQUY FOR NABOTH: 1 Kings 21: 1-29

SMALL QUESTIONS: The large questions referred to would be "To be or not to be" and "Death, where is thy sting?"

CHOICES: This poem was part of a give-and-take poetry therapy experiment.

MOURNING AFTER: It should be read aloud in a drunken slur.

THEY USED TO TELL: The trumpeter on my mind when I wrote this was Buddy Bolden.

THEY: This was written after reading many poems by Paul Celan.

LOREN KELLER, a teacher, writer, and actor, was born in Lancaster, NY in 1930, and has always lived in the Buffalo area. He has four children and nine grandchildren. After three years as an infantry lieutenant in the Korean War, he graduated from Buffalo State, where he won the Poetry Prize and the Essay Award. He continued his education at Cornell, Canisius, SUNY Buffalo, and California. During his 31 years as a teacher of Literature, English and Humanities and as Department Chairman in the Kenmore public schools, he was awarded a Ford Foundation Fellowship to the University of California at Berkeley in 1964, where he worked closely with the poet Gary Snyder.

Loren has published four previous books of poetry: *No Songs But Whispers* (1969), *The Skier and the Snow* (1978), *Warm Brooms* (1979) and *As I Might Hold A Bird* (1983). A book in collaboration with the artist Robert Freeland will be in print soon, entitled *The Shore You Reach*. Since the '80's, Loren has been the Playwright-in-Residence at Buffalo Ensemble Theatre, where five of his plays were produced: in 1986, *What Dreams May Come*, which was also performed in NY City (ten years before Robyn Williams used the same title), the play based on his experiences as a volunteer counselor for ten years at the former Suicide Prevention Center, now Crisis Services; in 1990, *No Spartan Shield*; in October 1991, *First Snow, Last Snow*; in 2001, an adaptation of *The Gift of the Magi*; in 2002, an adaptation of *It's a Wonderful Life*. His play *Walt Whitman, Oscar Wilde* was given a staged reading in Los Angeles.

As an actor he has appeared in many productions spanning five decades, including *The Elephant Man, The Dresser, The Runner Stumbles, Of Mice and Men* and *The Night of the Iguana*. He received the Best Actor award for his performance in *On Golden Pond*. For the past six years he has been a judge for a writing contest on Holocaust themes. His novel, *Four and Twenty Bluebeards* was published as a paperback and an AudioBook (read by the author) in 1999. He is a regular contributor to the literary magazine *First Intensity*, writing essays and reviews. Loren has donated substantial parts of his great book collection to the Medaille College library.